Devotions
On the
Run

Jim Burns

Regal

From Gospel Light
Ventura, California, U.S.A.

PUBLISHED BY REGAL BOOKS
FROM GOSPEL LIGHT
VENTURA, CALIFORNIA, U.S.A.
PRINTED IN THE U.S.A.

Regal Books is a ministry of Gospel Light, a Christian publisher dedicated to serving the local church. We believe God's vision for Gospel Light is to provide church leaders with biblical, user-friendly materials that will help them evangelize, disciple and minister to children, youth and families.

It is our prayer that this Regal book will help you discover biblical truth for your own life and help you meet the needs of others. May God richly bless you.

For a free catalog of resources from Regal Books/Gospel Light, please call your Christian supplier or contact us at 1-800-4-GOSPEL *or* www.regalbooks.com.

Parts of this book were originally printed in Jim Burns, *Spirit Wings* (Ann Arbor, MI: Servant Books, 1992).

The author has researched and attempted to fully attribute all quotes and illustrations in this book. Any inaccuracies or omissions are unintentional. All corrections from original sources or copyright holders should be directed to the publisher.

Cover design by David Griffing
Edited by Steven Lawson

LIBRARY OF CONGRESS CATALOGING-IN-PUBLICATION DATA

Burns, Jim, 1953–
    Devotions on the run / Jim Burns.
        p. cm.
    Rev. ed. of: Spirit wings. c1992.
    Includes bibliographical references.
    ISBN 0-8307-3330-2
    1. Youth—Prayer-books and devotions—English. I. Burns, Jim, 1953– Spirit wings. II. Title.
    BV4850.B855 1992
    242'.2—dc22   2004006220

1   2   3   4   5   6   7   8   9   10   /   10   09   08   07   06   05   04

Rights for publishing this book in other languages are contracted by Gospel Light Worldwide, the international nonprofit ministry of Gospel Light. Gospel Light Worldwide also provides publishing and technical assistance to international publishers dedicated to producing Sunday School and Vacation Bible School curricula and books in the languages of the world. For additional information, visit www.gospellightworldwide.org; write to Gospel Light Worldwide, P.O. Box 3875, Ventura, CA 93006; or send an e-mail to info@gospellightworldwide.org.

DEDICATION

TO RANDY AND SUSAN BRAMEL

You are two of the most inspiring people I have ever known.
You are friends, board members, mentors, heroes and incredible role models of what it means to be a Christ-follower. Thank
you for your sacrifice of time, talent and treasure to
YouthBuilders. You both are blessings.

CONTENTS

WEEK 1
The Great Decision

SUNDAY
The Courage to Pray

MONDAY
The Choosing of Christ

TUESDAY
No Greater Love

WEDNESDAY
The Love of Jesus

THURSDAY
This Is the Day

FRIDAY
The Source of Power

SATURDAY
The Delight of God

WEEK 2
A Loving God

SUNDAY
The Greatness of God

MONDAY
The Passion of God

TUESDAY
A Meditation

WEDNESDAY
A Sacrificial Love

THURSDAY
The Care of God

FRIDAY
Praise and Worship

SATURDAY
A Standing O

WEEK 3
An Insanely Generous Gift

SUNDAY
The Ultimate Christmas Present

MONDAY
The Lord Who Heals

TUESDAY
The Holy Spirit

WEDNESDAY
Set Free!

THURSDAY
Great Joy

FRIDAY
God Provides

SATURDAY
Big Power

WEEK 4
Ordinary People Doing Extraordinary Things

SUNDAY
Faith Is

MONDAY
Giving to Others

TUESDAY
Extraordinary Love

WEDNESDAY
God Knows What He Is Doing!

THURSDAY
A Great Story

FRIDAY
God Can Use You

SATURDAY
The Power of Affirmation

WEEK 5
Changing the Way You Think

SUNDAY
Getting Your Priorities Straight

MONDAY
Attitude and Circumstance

TUESDAY
Making People Brand New

WEDNESDAY
Hold That Criticism

THURSDAY
Living Beyond the Circumstance

FRIDAY
Living in the Fast Lane

SATURDAY
Checking Your Attitude

WEEK 6
Keeping Your Focus

SUNDAY
Taking Lessons from the Master

MONDAY
Pressing On

TUESDAY
What Will You Do With Jesus?

WEDNESDAY
Obedience

THURSDAY
Never Give Up!

FRIDAY
Go for It

SATURDAY
Waiting

WEEK 7
Getting It Together

SUNDAY
Standing at the Door

MONDAY
Put God First

TUESDAY
New Life

WEDNESDAY
New Beginnings

THURSDAY
Making Peace

FRIDAY
Don't Stop—Don't Quit

SATURDAY
Mending the Broken Parts

Acknowledgments

Special thanks to

Kelly Marie McFadden, for your friendship, "14 hours of inspiration" on this project, and for loaning me your dad and mom to help make a difference.

Judy Hedgren, for your servant's heart and the kindness you bring to YouthBuilders.

Bob Campbell, for speaking into my life, giving so much of yourself and causing me to dream big.

Todd Dean, for your wonderful leadership.

Mary Perdue, for being one of the finest people of encouragement I have ever met.

Dean Bruns, for your friendship, longevity to the YouthBuilders vision and being a team player.

Mindy Di Nicola, for your enthusiasm and faithful consistency to your job.

Kim Dixon, for your prayer life and the way you serve YouthBuilders.

Jim Liebelt, for your years of dedication and help.

Becca Burns, for being the coolest (and youngest) employee at YouthBuilders.

PREFACE

Taking a few minutes to spend time with God and focus on His will for your life is the most important thing you can do today. Some days you will be preoccupied with urgent issues. The saying is true: If the Devil can't make you bad, then he will make you busy. If your life is too busy to take a few minutes with God each day, then your life is just too busy.

Devotions on the Run was created to help you get into the habit of regularly spending time with God. To get started, take just 10 minutes a day with God for the next 49 days. Each devotional reading includes a Scripture, a story or a thought, a section for going deeper and a psalm. The thoughts are designed to give you a boost and a focus for your day. The devotions are not necessarily the deepest ever written; rather, in the simplicity of each message you will find something to reflect on. Many families read these devotions at the beginning of the day or at the dinner table. If you are one of the more than 1 million people who hear our YouthBuilders one-minute radio spots each day, you may recognize some of the stories. Most of all, this book was written for you to find the strength and encouragement to focus on God and to enable you to make the most out of each day.

THE GREAT DECISION

Then he called the crowd to him along with his disciples and said: "If anyone would come after me, he must deny himself and take up his cross and follow me."

MARK 8:34

9/28

THE COURAGE TO PRAY

Examine me, O God, and know my mind; test me, and discover my thoughts.
Find out if there is any evil in me and guide me in the everlasting way.

PSALM 139:23-24

Have you ever prayed a life-changing prayer? Maybe it was a time when you were wrestling with an issue that you knew was wrong, but could release it to God only after some struggle.

When I was 16, I made a commitment to follow Jesus and asked Him into my heart. Until that time athletics, especially baseball, was the main focus of my life. I thought I would be a professional baseball player. After becoming a Christian, I sensed God wanted me to go into the ministry instead. My struggle was between something I loved doing and what I believed that God was leading me to do. One day, as I sat on the sand at the beach looking at the Pacific Ocean, I prayed a life-changing prayer. It went something like this: "God, I surrender my will to Yours. I will go wherever You want and do whatever Your desire is for my life. After all, You know more about me than I do." Instantly I felt a sense of release and peace. God was in control. That, I believe, was the day that God led me into a life of full-time Christian service, and I have never regretted a single moment of it.

Are you willing to pray a life-changing prayer? It can go something like this: "LORD, I'm willing to go anywhere and do anything for You." When you do pray that prayer, be assured that God has His best in mind for you.

FURTHER FATHOMS

- Have you ever prayed a life-changing prayer? What was the result? *I married Laura!*
- Read Psalm 139:23-24 again. Write out several issues *Kevin!* that God is impressing upon you. Do you have the *Yes I am praying* courage to pray a life-changing prayer for these issues?

POWERFUL PRAISES

Seek your happiness in the LORD, and he will give you your heart's desire.

PSALM 37:4

You created every part of me; you put me together in my mother's womb. I praise you because you are to be feared; all you do is strange and wonderful. I know it with all my heart.

PSALM 139:13-14

RAPID RECAP

- Thank God.
- Listen to what He is saying to you today.

THE CHOOSING OF CHRIST

*Then he called the crowd to him along with his disciples
and said: "If anyone would come after me, he must deny himself
and take up his cross and follow me."*

MARK 8:34

Dan worked in the inner city of Chicago. He dedicated his life to helping poor kids find meaning through Jesus Christ. Dan had a friend, Enrique. At 13, Enrique had never been out of the city and he belonged to a gang. Enrique never knew who his father was, and his mother wasn't citizen of the year.

Dan took Enrique and three other boys to Wisconsin for a weekend Christian retreat. Enrique had never been to church before. When he heard that God loved him unconditionally not for what he did but for who he was—a child of God—Enrique jumped at the chance to become a Christian. Dan was excited.

When the group traveled home from the camp, Dan noticed Enrique looked very nervous. "What's wrong?" he asked.

"Tonight I have to run the gauntlet," was Enrique's reply.

"What do you mean?" Dan asked.

"Basically, I'm going to get beat up real bad."

"What are you talking about, Enrique?"

"When you leave a gang, the gang members line up on both sides in a row with clubs, bats, rings and their fists. You run the gauntlet and they give you a beating you'll remember the rest of your life."

"Why do you have to run the gauntlet tonight?"

Enrique looked at Dan and matter-of-factly said, "Dan, I can't have Jesus and the gang. I've decided I want Jesus more than I want to be in the gang."

FURTHER FATHOMS

- What inspires you about Enrique's newfound faith in Christ?
- What specifically does it mean to your life to deny yourself, take up your cross and follow Christ?

POWERFUL PRAISE

May those who want to see me acquitted shout for joy and say again and again, "How great is the LORD! He is pleased with the success of his servant." Then I will proclaim your righteousness, and I will praise you all day long.

PSALM 35:27-28

RAPID RECAP

- Make a choice.
- Pick up your cross and follow Jesus.

NO GREATER LOVE

Greater love has no one than this, that he lay down his life for his friends.

JOHN 15:13

Dan went with Enrique to meet with the gang leaders. They walked to a broken-down basketball court where the gang members hung out. Enrique spoke first. With fear in his eyes and a quivering voice, he told the leader of the gang he needed to run the gauntlet.

"Why, Enrique? What's wrong?"

Enrique looked at Dan and then at his fellow gang members. His reply was so simple: "I asked Jesus into my heart and I know I've got to leave the gang."

"Enrique," the gang leader implored. "Let me give you a second chance. You don't want to run the gauntlet, but you'll need to give up this Jesus stuff."

Enrique looked again at Dan and then replied, "I've made up my mind."

The gang leader shrugged his shoulders and said, "OK, the gauntlet it is."

Dan then looked straight into the gang leader's eyes and said, "About this gauntlet business, is there any way to convince you not to hurt Enrique?"

The gang leader laughed and just shook his head, "No. Absolutely not."

Dan cleared his throat and said, "Then I'd like to take Enrique's place." There was complete silence from the gang leader. He had probably never heard anything like this from anyone, let alone a white youth worker who had moved to the inner city from upper-middle-class suburbia.

At first the gang leader was speechless. Then he smiled, "Let me check with the others."

Enrique knew his gang leader would like nothing more than to beat Dan within an inch of his life. Enrique and Dan stood in silence as the others discussed the proposition before them. Dan had volunteered to take Enrique's place. Finally, after much discussion the gang leader came back. Without even looking at Dan he told Enrique, "You can change your mind, but if you don't you'll run the gauntlet at 9:00 tonight."

He then turned and walked away.

Enrique looked at Dan. "Would you really have done that for me?"

Dan put his arm around Enrique and said, "Of course I would."

A tear appeared on Enrique's cheek, his big brown eyes, now moist, looked up at his friend. All he could say was "Thanks."

FURTHER FATHOMS

- Dan was willing to run the gauntlet for Enrique. How does Dan's faith challenge you?
- Read John 15:13 again. Write a thank-you note to Christ for laying down His life on the cross for you.

POWERFUL PRAISE

It is good to sing praise to our God; it is pleasant and right to praise him. The LORD is restoring Jerusalem; he is bringing back the exiles. He heals the broken-hearted and bandages their wounds. He has decided the number of the stars and calls each one by name. Great and mighty is our LORD; his wisdom cannot be measured. He raises the humble, but crushes the wicked to the ground. His pleasure is not in strong horses, nor his delight in brave soldiers; but he takes pleasure in those who honor him, in those who trust in his constant love.

PSALM 147:1-6,10-11

RAPID RECAP

- Count the cost of following Christ.
- Thank Jesus for what He has done for you today.

THE LOVE OF JESUS

For Christ died for sins once for all, the righteous for the unrighteous, to bring you to God. He was put to death in the body but made alive by the Spirit.

1 PETER 3:18

At 9:05 p.m., Enrique's gang members lined up in two rows holding bats and clubs, cussing and screaming obscenities. They called this 13-year-old boy a sissy for turning to Jesus. Dan and Enrique stood side by side—each wore a horrified look. Dan kept asking, "Is this really happening?" Enrique looked up at Dan and needed reassurance once more. "Dan, you're absolutely sure Jesus loves me?" Dan, checking every motive in his life, said, "He loved you so much He was willing to go to the cross and die for the forgiveness of your sins and mine." Dan knew there was a possibility that Enrique was going to his cross for his now two-day-old faith in Jesus.

The leader yelled, "Go for it, Enrique." Dan watched as his little friend got slugged, hit and kicked. Dan will never forget the picture imprinted on his mind of this terrible beating. Dan had begged, screamed, pleaded, prayed and threatened. Now Enrique was curled up in a ball protecting himself from the blows to every part of his body.

At last the gang leader called it off. Enrique lay still, bloody and bruised. He couldn't speak and he couldn't walk. Dan carried Enrique in his arms 12 blocks to the nearest hospital. They waited three hours for help. Enrique's head was badly cut. His shoulder was already swollen and two teeth were entirely missing. His groin had swollen to the size of a grapefruit.

Finally, a nurse put Enrique on a gurney and wheeled him to the emergency room. Dan walked quietly at his side. In the elevator, Enrique looked up through his bloodshot eyes, and said, "Jesus really does love me, doesn't He?" Dan smiled. Enrique—whose own face was bruised—added, "He went through extreme pain, even death for me, right?" Dan nodded. "Then I'm glad I could go through this for my Savior," Enrique quietly concluded.

FURTHER FATHOMS

- This is a powerful true story. How does it challenge you?
- How is Enrique's commitment similar to the sacrifice of Christ on the cross?

POWERFUL PRAISE

Praise the LORD! Praise the LORD from heaven, you that live in the heights above. Praise him, all his angels, all his heavenly armies. Praise him, sun and moon; praise him, shining stars. Praise him, highest heavens, and the waters above the sky. Let them all praise the name of the LORD! He commanded, and they were created; by his command they were fixed in their places forever, and they cannot disobey. Praise the LORD from the earth, sea monsters and all ocean depths; lightening and hail, snow and clouds, strong winds that obey his command. Praise him, hills and mountains, fruit trees and forests; all animals, tame and wild, reptiles and birds. Praise him, kings and all peoples, princes and all other rulers;

young women and young men, old people and children too. Let them all praise the name of the LORD! His name is greater than all others; his glory is above earth and heaven. He made his nation strong, so that all his people praise him—the people of Israel, so dear to him. Praise the LORD!

PSALM 148

RAPID RECAP

- Jesus sacrificed all on the cross.
- What can you go through for Jesus today?

THIS IS THE DAY

So whether you eat or drink or whatever you do, do it all for the glory of God.

1 CORINTHIANS 10:31

If you live to be 70 years old, on average you will spend

- 20 years sleeping
- 16 years working
- 7 years playing
- 6 years eating
- 5 years dressing (4 1/2 years for bald-headed men like me!)
- 3 years waiting for somebody
- 1 1/2 years in church
- 1 year on the telephone
- 5 months tying your shoes

How are you spending your time? Are you productively making a positive difference with your life? Everything you do can be done with an attitude of thankfulness and praise. You can choose to make it a wonderful day with God. Go for it!

FURTHER FATHOMS

- What can you do with your time today that will make a positive difference in your life?

- What do 1 Corinthians 10:31 and Colossians 3:17 mean specifically for your life?

POWERFUL PRAISE

This is the day of the LORD's victory; let us be happy, let us celebrate!

PSALM 118:24

RAPID RECAP

- You have 24 hours today.
- It is important to God how we spend our time.

THE SOURCE OF POWER

And I will ask the Father, and he will give you another Counselor to be with you forever—the Spirit of truth. The world cannot accept him, because it neither sees him nor knows him. But you know him, for he lives with you and will be in you.

JOHN 14:16-17

But I tell you the truth: It is for your good that I am going away. Unless I go away, the Counselor will not come to you; but if I go, I will send him to you.

JOHN 16:7

The Holy Spirit is the third person of the Trinity. He is very much on the same level in the Trinity as the Father and as Jesus. His role in the Godhead (Trinity) is different from the roles of the Father and of Jesus. The Father is the creator and the Son (Jesus) is the Savior. The Spirit is the counselor and comforter.

The Holy Spirit's job is to empower and guide you in living the Christian life. In order to have the power of God working in your life you must surrender and submit to the control of the Holy Spirit. You can surrender and submit to the Holy Spirit simply by asking Him to fill you with His presence.

Here is a prayer I pray regularly. I hope it will be your prayer today as well.

Spirit of the living God, take control of me; Spirit of the living God, take control of me; Spirit of the living God, take control of me; Melt me! Mold me! Fill me! Use me!

Asking the Holy Spirit to fill, empower and control your life connects you with the power source of God. It is putting God in the driver's seat of your life with you in the passenger seat. If you make this commitment, hold on because you are in for the greatest, most exciting and challenging ride of your life.

Are you ready?

FURTHER FATHOMS

- What is the incredibly good news in today's Scriptures?
- Has there ever been a time in your life when you have prayed a prayer like the one I pray? Yes? When and how has it affected your life? No? Then why not make that the prayer of your heart today?

POWERFUL PRAISE

I have complete confidence, O God! I will sing and praise you! Wake up, my soul! Wake up, my harp and lyre! I will wake up the sun. I will thank you, O LORD, among the nations. I will praise you among the peoples. Your constant love reaches above the heavens; your faithfulness touches the skies. Show your greatness in the sky, O God, and your glory over all the earth.

PSALM 108:1-5

RAPID RECAPS

- The Holy Spirit is your power source.
- Pray for Him to fill you and use you.

THE DELIGHT OF GOD

Trust in the LORD with all your heart and lean not on your own understanding; in all your ways acknowledge him, and he will make your paths straight.

PROVERBS 3:5-6

I live near the beach. Because of the action of the waves and the constant movement of the water, the ocean is never stagnant. On the other hand, right by my house there is a water hole. When it rains, the water hole grows bigger, but because there is no outlet for the water, it quickly stagnates. Inside the water, you can see all kinds of parasites and fungus. In fact, only a few days after the rain the water hole begins to smell real bad.

Our faith in Jesus is no different. Faith is acting out our belief in God. Faith is action. Faith is never stagnant. When we act upon our beliefs, good things will happen; when we remain stagnant, our faith does not grow. Here are some important principles from today's psalm of praise:

Trust in God and do good = safe living
Delight in God = receiving the true desires of your heart
Commit your way to God = your life will shine

With these principles and results for our faith, is there really any better way to live than a life of faith in action? Put your faith, your trust and your life in the hands of God—and watch the results.

FURTHER FATHOMS

- Are there areas in your life that are stagnant and not led by faith?
- Trusting, delighting and committing are action steps to faith. How can you make these more real in your life?

POWERFUL PRAISE

Trust in the LORD and do good; live in the land and be safe. Seek your happiness in the LORD, and he will give you your heart's desire. Give yourself to the LORD; trust in him, and he will help you.

PSALM 37:3-5

RAPID RECAPS

- Trust in the LORD.
- Delight in His name.

A LOVING GOD

*Amen! Praise and glory and wisdom and thanks and honor and power
and strength be to our God for ever and ever. Amen!*

REVELATION 7:12

THE GREATNESS OF GOD

For God so loved the world that he gave his one and only Son, that whoever believes in him shall not perish but have eternal life.

JOHN 3:16

Martin Luther once called John 3:16, "The heart of the Bible— the Gospel in miniature."[1] This verse is one of the most famous verses in all of Scripture. It condenses the deep and marvelous truths of our faith into these incredible words:

God	The greatest lover
so loved	The greatest degree
the world	The greatest number
that He gave	The greatest act
His one and only Son	The greatest gift
that whoever	The greatest invitation
believes	The greatest simplicity
in Him	The greatest person
shall not perish	The greatest deliverance
but have	The greatest certainty
eternal life	The greatest possession

FURTHER FATHOMS

- Why is John 3:16 such good news to you personally?
- How did today's devotional inspire you?
- Repeat this phrase out loud five times: God gave His Son to die for me. As you repeat it, think about the magnitude of what you are saying.

POWERFUL PRAISE

I rely on your constant love; I will be glad, because you will rescue me. I will sing to you, O LORD, because you have been good to me.

PSALM 13:5-6

RAPID RECAP

- John 3:16 is the gospel in miniature.
- God is great.

THE PASSION OF GOD

*God demonstrates his own love for us in this: While we were
still sinners, Christ died for us.*

ROMANS 5:8

I often think about passion. No, not the kind of passion that is
available on movie screens, the type of passion far too many
Hollywood types promote. I'm thinking about the kind of passion
my surfer friend Rick has for the perfect wave. Up at 4:30 in the
morning, he drives to the beach, looking for the best swell. Out in
the water waiting, watching, he finds it. Ready, steady, he takes it.
Oooh, it was worth the inconvenience of too little sleep and too
cold water.

Personally, I have a passion for Italian food; vacations; my wife,
Cathy; my daughters; a walk on the beach; snorkeling; Häagen-Dazs
cookies-and-cream ice cream; youth ministry and God. Sometimes
I will drive 15 miles out of my way for a double scoop of Häagen-
Dazs or work extra days, weeks and months to afford a vacation on
the beach in Hawaii where I can go snorkeling. Passion usually
involves a deep love and a deep sacrifice for something or someone.

What's your passion? What do you think about during the
day and dream about at night? What are you willing to love

deeply and sacrificially?

I wonder for a moment what is the passion of God. Then the answer comes to me. You and I are the passion of God. God has a one track mind. He loves us. He created us. He gives us life and breath. He brings us new life through the sacrificial death of Jesus.

With His love and His Holy Spirit, he passionately pursues us. Isn't it nice to know beyond a shadow of a doubt that we are loved with the passion of God?

FURTHER FATHOMS

- When was there a time in your life that you passionately pursued God? When was there a time that you felt like God's passionate love was pursuing you?
- Reread Romans 5:8. Would you die for someone who betrayed you?

POWERFUL PRAISE

Sing to the LORD, all the world! Worship the LORD with joy; come before him with happy songs! Acknowledge that the LORD is God. He made us, and we belong to him; we are his people, we are his flock. Enter the Temple gates with thanksgiving; go into its courts with praise. Give thanks to him and praise him. The LORD is good; his love is eternal and his faithfulness lasts forever.

PSALM 100

RAPID RECAP

- God is passionately pursuing you right now.
- He wants you to love Him with passion.

A MEDITATION

Love must be sincere. Hate what is evil; cling to what is good. Be devoted to one another in brotherly love. Honor one another above yourselves. Never be lacking in zeal, but keep your spiritual fervor, serving the LORD. Be joyful in hope, patient in affliction, faithful in prayer. Share with God's people who are in need. Practice hospitality. Bless those who persecute you; bless and do not curse. Rejoice with those who rejoice; mourn with those who mourn. Live in harmony with one another. Do not be proud, but be willing to associate with people of low position. Do not be conceited.

ROMANS 12: 9-16

If you are under 40 years of age, you may not remember Cary Grant. He was an actor and superstar in every sense of the word. In his later years, he made occasional appearances in theaters around the United States billed simply as "A Conversation with Cary Grant." He didn't need much advertising; one small ad would appear in the local newspaper and the theater would immediately sell out. Everywhere he appeared, he received a standing ovation when he walked onto the stage.

At the end of each performance he always read a meditation, saying he didn't know who wrote it but that the words also expressed his feelings about life. I like it very much and offer it to you today:

Now LORD, you've known me a long time. You know me better than I know myself. You now that each day I am growing older and someday may even be very old, so meanwhile please keep me from the habit of thinking I must say something on every subject and on every occasion.

Release me from trying to straighten out everyone's affairs. Make me thoughtful but not moody, helpful but not overbearing. I've a certain amount of knowledge to share, still it would be very nice to have a few friends who, at the end, recognized and forgave the knowledge I lacked.

Keep my tongue free from the recital of endless details. Seal my lips on my aches and pains: They increase daily and the need to speak of them becomes almost a compulsion. I ask for grace enough to listen to the retelling of others' afflictions, and to be helped to endure them with patience.

I would like to have improved memory, but I'll settle for growing humility and an ability to capitulate when my memory clashes with the memory of others. Teach me the glorious lesson that on some occasions, I may be mistaken.

Keep me reasonably kind; I've never aspired to be a saint, saints must be rather difficult to live with yet, on the other hand, an embittered old person is a constant burden.

Please give me the ability to see good in unlikely places and talents in unexpected people. And give me the grace to tell them so, dear LORD.[1]

Romans 12:9-16 and Cary Grant's meditation summarize a lifestyle that is humble, balanced and focused. Take a moment to think about what areas in your life need your silence, love or help. I bet you can find at least one. I sure can in my own life!

FURTHER FATHOMS

- What point in Cary Grant's meditation strikes you the most?
- Paraphrase Romans 12:9-16. Ask God to help you to live out Psalm 128:1-2 in your life this week.

POWERFUL PRAISE

Happy are those who obey the LORD, who live by his commands. You work will provide for your needs; you will be happy and prosperous.

PSALM 128:1-2

RAPID RECAP

- God wants us to be humble, balanced and focused.
- God can act when we are silent.

A SACRIFICIAL LOVE

It was now about the sixth hour, and darkness came over the whole land until the ninth hour, for the sun stopped shining. And the curtain of the temple was torn in two. Jesus called out with a loud voice, "Father, into your hands I commit my spirit." When he had said this, he breathed his last. The centurion, seeing what had happened, praised God and said, "Surely this was a righteous man." When all the people who had gathered to witness this sight saw what took place, they beat their breasts and went away. But all those who knew him, including the women who had followed him from Galilee, stood at a distance, watching these things.

LUKE 23:44-49

And I asked Jesus, "LORD, do you really love me?" And His reply was, "Yes, I really do love you." "But just how much do you love me, LORD?" I inquired. And He said, "This much." Then He stretched out His hands and died. There is something about the sacrificial love of Jesus Christ that keeps me focused on my faith. "But God demonstrates his own love for us in this: While we were still sinners, Christ died for us" (Rom. 5:8).

There is something about the blood, the mocking, the abandonment and the cross that puts life and the love of God in perspective.

FURTHER FATHOMS

- Take a few minutes to read Luke 22–24. It is the story of the betrayal, arrest, mocking, crucifixion, death, burial and resurrection of Jesus.
- How does the sacrificial love of Jesus for you affect your faith?

POWERFUL PRAISE

An evil gang is around me; like a pack of dogs they close in on me; they tear at my hands and feet. All my bones can be seen. My enemies look at me and stare. They gamble for my clothes and divide them among themselves. O Lord, don't stay away from me! Come quickly to my rescue! Save me from the sword; save my life from these dogs. Rescue me from these lions; I am helpless before these wild bulls. I will tell my people what you have done; I will praise you in their assembly: "Praise him, you servants of the Lord! Honor him, you descendants of Jacob! Worship him, you people of Israel! He does not neglect the poor or ignore their suffering; he does not turn away from them, but answers when they call for help." In the full assembly I will praise you for what you have done; in the presence of those who worship you I will offer the sacrifices I promised

PSALM 22:16-25

RAPID RECAP

- True love makes sacrifices.
- Jesus made the ultimate sacrifice.

THE CARE OF GOD

The LORD himself goes before you and will be with you; he will never leave you nor forsake you. Do not be afraid; do not be discouraged.

DEUTERONOMY 31:8

How close is God? God is closer than your breath and closer than your skin. Philippians 4:5 reminds you to never forget the nearness of your God. How much does he care for you?

- He knows your name (see John 10:3).
- He numbers the hairs on your head (see Matt. 10:30).
- He counts the steps of your feet (see Job 14:16).
- He bottles the tears from your eyes (see Ps. 56:8, *RSV*).
- He holds your right hand in His hand (see Ps. 73:23).
- He supplies all of your needs (see Phil. 4:19).

It is easy to act like a child lost in a theme park. Do you ever feel alone in a world surrounded by millions of faces? You reach out and look for someone to really know you, to really care. But in time you tend to isolate yourself in your own worries and cry until help arrives. Do not be discouraged. God is with you and God goes before you. He knows and understands your problems and concerns. In fact, He cares! The question then becomes Will you let Him care?

FURTHER FATHOMS

- Try counting the hairs on your head (no fair if you are bald!). Now are you convinced God knows everything about you?
- Memorize Deuteronomy 31:8. Why is it helpful to know this verse by heart?
- List five struggles in your life and then write out how today's devotional applies to each of them.

POWERFUL PRAISE

The LORD is merciful and good; our God is compassionate. The LORD protects the helpless; when I was in danger, he saved me. Be confident, my heart, because the LORD has been good to me. What can I offer the LORD for all his goodness to me? I will bring a wine offering to the LORD, to thank him for saving me. In the assembly of all his people I will give him what I have promised.

PSALM 116:5-7,12-14

RAPID RECAP

- God knows everything about you.
- He still cares!

PRAISE AND WORSHIP

*Praise be to the God and Father of our LORD Jesus Christ, who has blessed us
in the heavenly realms with every spiritual blessing in Christ. For he chose us in
him before the creation of the world to be holy and blameless in his sight. In love
he predestined us to be adopted as his sons through Jesus Christ, in accordance
with his pleasure and will—to the praise of his glorious grace, which he has freely
given us in the One he loves. In him we have redemption through his blood, the
forgiveness of sins, in accordance with the riches of God's grace that he lavished
on us with all wisdom and understanding. And he made known to us the mys-
tery of his will according to his good pleasure, which he purposed in Christ, to be
put into effect when the times will have reached their fulfillment—to bring all
things in heaven and on earth together under one head, even Christ. In him we
were also chosen, having been predestined according to the plan of him who
works out everything in conformity with the purpose of his will, in order that we,
who were the first to hope in Christ, might be for the praise of his glory. And you
also were included in Christ when you heard the word of truth, the gospel of your
salvation. Having believed, you were marked in him with a seal, the promised
Holy Spirit, who is a deposit guaranteeing our inheritance until the redemption
of those who are God's possession—to the praise of his glory.*

EPHESIANS 1:3-14

When you praise the LORD, you unleash the Spirit of God to
do awesome acts of power. Here are a few reasons why my
heart is filled with praise and worship to the King of kings.

Can you praise Him, too?

- Praise God for the beauty of his creation (see Ps. 19).
- Praise God for the power of the Holy Spirit (see Acts 1:8).
- Praise God for the blood of Christ for redemption (see Rev. 5:9).
- Praise God for healing the broken-hearted (see Ps. 147:3).
- Praise God for His birth: Emmanuel (see Luke 2)
- Praise God for His life on Earth (see John 3:15-17).
- Praise God for the cross and sacrificial love (see Rom. 5:8).
- Praise God for His mighty works (see Deut. 3:24).
- Praise God for His mighty acts of power (see Ps. 150:2).
- Praise God for His Word (see 1 Pet. 1:24-25).

Praise is music to God's ears. God inhabits praise. God loves to hear His children offer Him praise. How can you make God happy? Praise Him! Why should God be praised? He is your creator, redeemer and comforter.

Praise releases the power of God. Praise is an expression of gratitude for His mighty acts of power and His surpassing greatness. Praise releases your life into the hands of God. Praise releases the Holy Spirit within you to call upon His almighty authority. Praise releases your spirit to sing of His awesome greatness!

FURTHER FATHOMS

- Make a list of reasons why you are filled with praise today.
- Take a minute to sing a song of praise to God. Now sing another one.

POWERFUL PRAISE

Come, praise the LORD, all his servants, all who serve in his Temple at night. Raise your hands in prayer in the Temple, and praise the LORD! May the LORD, who made heaven and earth, bless you from Zion!

PSALM 134

RAPID RECAP

- God inhabits praise.
- There is power in praise.

A STANDING O

Who shall separate us from the love of Christ? Shall trouble or hardship or persecution or famine or nakedness or danger or sword? As it is written: "For your sake we face death all day long; we are considered as sheep to be slaughtered." No, in all these things we are more than conquerors through him who loved us.

ROMANS 8:35-37

It had been one of those crummy days. I walked off the platform of a high school auditorium, feeling depressed and dejected. I did not connect with the kids. In fact, what I thought would work at the assembly fell flat. I mumbled an apology to the principal and walked to my car, feeling broken and downcast. The entire day, I let this bomb of an assembly get to me.

That night my sleep was interrupted by a dream (I believe God gave me this dream). I found myself in the same auditorium as I had been in earlier in the day. It was empty except for one person sitting in the front row—Jesus. As I walked to the platform, Jesus rose to his feet and gave me a standing ovation! He cheered, whistled and applauded with enthusiasm before I even spoke.

When I awoke I remember smiling so big that my face hurt. God loves me, not for what I do, but for who I am—His child. Did you catch that? God loves you, too—not for what you do, but for who you are—His child.

Did you know Jesus daily gives you a standing ovation? He loved you enough to die for you. I have this feeling that if He carries a wallet in heaven, your picture and mine are in that wallet. Isn't it nice to be loved?

FURTHER FATHOMS

- When was there a time in your life when you could have used a standing ovation from God?
- How do you feel when you read Romans 8:35-37?

POWERFUL PRAISE

The LORD is my shepherd; I have everything I need. He lets me rest in fields of green grass and leads me to quiet pools of fresh water. He gives me new strength. He guides me in the right paths, as he has promised. Even if I go through the deepest darkness, I will not be afraid, LORD, for you are with me. Your shepherd's rod and staff protect me. You prepare a banquet for me, where all my enemies can see me; you welcome me as an honored guest and fill my cup to the brim. I know that your goodness and love will be with me all my life; and your house will be my home as long as I live.

PSALM 23

RAPID RECAP

- God loves you because you are His child.
- God is with you even when you have a bad day.

WEEK 3

AN INSANELY GENEROUS GIFT

This is love: not that we loved God, but that he loved us and sent his Son as an atoning sacrifice for our sins.

1 JOHN 4:10

THE ULTIMATE CHRISTMAS PRESENT

And there were shepherds living out in the fields nearby, keeping watch over their flocks at night. An angel of the LORD appeared to them, and the glory of the LORD shone around them, and they were terrified. But the angel said to them, "Do not be afraid. I bring you good news of great joy that will be for all the people. Today in the town of David a Savior has been born to you; he is Christ the LORD. This will be a sign to you: You will find a baby wrapped in cloths and lying in a manger." Suddenly a great company of the heavenly host appeared with the angel, praising God and saying, "Glory to God in the highest, and on earth peace to men on whom his favor rests."

LUKE 2:8-14

Daniel was born with a degenerative heart condition. This problem was in remission for most of his childhood and teen years. He lived a normal kid's life filled with friends, baseball and drama. But in his junior year of high school, he had massive heart failure. By late 1980, he had spent several months at Stanford Medical Center, in what is called Life Row. He was waiting for a heart transplant. On December 22 the doctors sent Daniel home for Christmas, expecting him to die before they could find a heart for him. But he was immediately rushed back to the hospital because they had a heart donor, and at age 17, Daniel had a successful heart-transplant operation.

Three days later on Christmas day, his mom read Luke 2 to Daniel while he was in recovery. Then she read the stacks of get-well cards from people all over the country who were praying for him. She pulled a card from the Midwest out of the pile and read the following note.

> Dear Daniel,
>
> Even though we do not know you, my husband and I feel so close to you and your family. Our only son, Lloyd, was your heart donor. Knowing that you have his heart has made our loss so much easier to bear. With all our love,
>
> Paul and Barbara Chambers[1]

Daniel wrote later about that experience:

> I couldn't fight the tears any longer. And suddenly I knew more clearly than ever the real reason why I should be celebrating Christmas. In dying, the Chambers's only son had given me life. In dying, God's only Son had given life, eternal life. Now I felt like shouting out loud my thanks that Jesus Christ was born!
>
> "Thank You, LORD!" I said. "And bless you," I said as I thought of the young man who had signed the donor card that gave me my greatest Christmas present of all, "Bless you, Lloyd Chambers."[2]

So often in life we are given gifts and don't realize the sacrifice that has been made for us to receive them. Take a moment to think about the cost of our greatest gift, Jesus Christ.

FURTHER FATHOMS

- If you were Daniel, what would your response be to that letter?
- What is the spiritual significance of today's devotional?

POWERFUL PRAISE

Praise God with shouts of joy, all people! Sing to the glory of his name; offer him glorious praise! Say to God, "How wonderful are the things you do! Your power is so great that your enemies bow down in fear before you. Everyone on earth worships you; they sing praises to you, they sing praises to your name." Come and see what God has done, his wonderful acts among people.

PSALM 66:1-5

RAPID RECAP

- Jesus Christ is God's greatest gift to us.
- Christ's greatest gift to us was His life.

THE LORD WHO HEALS

*[The LORD] said, "If you listen carefully to the voice of the LORD your God
and do what is right in his eyes, if you pay attention to his commands and keep
all his decrees, I will not bring on you any of the diseases I brought on the
Egyptians, for I am the LORD, who heals you."*

EXODUS 15:26

Our LORD has been called the Great Physician. One of the
names for God in the Old Testament is *Rapha*, meaning "the
LORD who heals."[1] Some of us in the Christian faith have mis-
understood God's job description as a healer. We know that
there are thousands of walking physical miracles that demon-
strate God's healing power. Cancer disappears, the lame walk
and sometimes the blind see. The way I read the Bible, we are
commanded by God to pray for the healing of the sick; sometimes—but not every time—there is an instantaneous healing.

I see the Great Physician the same way I see most modern-
day doctors. Doctors examine us, consult with us, work on us
and even oversee our rehabilitation. Rapha—God—has the same
job description, only on a much larger scale and He, of course, is
much more powerful.

- **God examines us.** He watches over us and searches out our every need.
- **God consults with us.** He guides our lives and, often through circumstances, gives us direction. He listens to our requests and responds.
- **God works on us.** Sometimes we need to be cut open and disciplined. He is constantly giving us help to become whole.
- **God oversees our rehabilitation.** Once we are on the way to wholeness and healing, He doesn't leave us but watches over us and protects our healing.

I don't know about you but I'm glad He is called Rapha, the LORD who heals.

FURTHER FATHOMS

- Describe a few situations in which you have experienced God as your healing physician.
- What do you think Exodus 15:26 really means?

POWERFUL PRAISE

Then in their trouble they called to the LORD, and he saved them from their distress. He healed them with his command and saved them from the grave. They must thank the LORD for his constant love, for the wonderful things he did for them. They must thank him with sacrifices, and with songs of joy must tell all that he has done.

PSALM 107:19-22

RAPID RECAP

- God is Rapha, our LORD who heals.
- Not only can God fix our bodies, but He also examines every detail of our lives.

THE HOLY SPIRIT

But you will receive power when the Holy Spirit comes on you; and you will be my witnesses in Jerusalem, and in all Judea and Samaria, and to the ends of the earth.

ACTS 1:8

In the early 1900s, many ships sank while attempting to wind their way through Hell's Gate—where the Harlem and East rivers converge in New York. Only vessels of a certain size could make their way up the treacherous river. General Richard Newton was given the task of making the passageway navigable.

General Newton and his crew spent several years building tunnels under the banks of the river. They then placed tons of dynamite in those tunnels. On the appointed day all ships and people were diverted.

The General sat in his home two miles away with his little daughter on his knee. At the appointed time, he told his daughter, "Press the black button." She did. In the distance there was a muffled roar. The water shot up 150 feet in the air and the river was cleared. From that point forward, ships could safely pass through this dangerous passage. The little child was powerless; but because of the genuine power of her illustrious father's work, when she pushed the tiny black button, she became powerful.[1]

We are helpless without the filling of the Holy Spirit, but with Him we are all powerful and nothing in hell can stop us.

FURTHER FATHOMS

- What is the message behind today's story?
- Have you ever asked God to fill and empower you with His Holy Spirit? If not, why not ask Him to do so right now?

POWERFUL PRAISE

The world and all that is in it belong to the LORD; the earth and all who live on it are his. He built it on the deep waters beneath the earth and laid its foundations in the ocean depths. Who is this great king? He is the LORD, strong and mighty, the LORD, victorious in battle. Fling wide the gates, open the ancient doors, and the great king will come in. Who is this great king? The triumphant LORD—he is the great king!

PSALM 24:1-2,8-10

RAPID RECAP

- Without God, we are helpless.
- With the power of His Holy Spirit, we can do all things.

SET FREE!

Then you will know the truth, and the truth will set you free.

JOHN 8:32

Erin looked happy on the outside. She was very pretty, she was a cheerleader, and she had lots of dates. What else could a seventeen-year-old want? Yet no one, absolutely no one, knew the deep agony of her soul. She often tried to forget what had occurred on those horrible nights not so long ago—but fear would set in. There were times when she tried alcohol to deaden her pain. But the booze only worked temporarily, and when she was sober, she hurt even more.

One day at a youth event called This Side Up, Erin heard a speaker talk about sexual abuse. He said, "If you have been sexually abused it's not your fault; it's the fault of the abuser." He went on to say, "Today is the day to seek help; please don't suffer in silence." The speaker went on to offer hope. For the first time in her life, she heard that God cares. If Jesus wept for the death of his friend Lazarus, then he weeps for people like Erin who have been abused.

Erin's story is far too common. For years, her stepfather molested her; but she told no one. At that youth conference, Erin got up the courage to seek out a counselor. For the first time, she shared her story.

The year that followed was not easy. Erin went to a treatment center and had to make several court appearances—and her stepfather eventually went to prison. Erin continued to seek out her Christian counselor on a regular basis to talk about her life. Finally, she asked Jesus Christ to come into her life and to fill her hurt and emptiness.

I asked Erin, "With all that has happened, do you wish you had never made the decision to seek help?" She looked at me and laughed. "To say it's been easy would be a lie, but I would not want to change one moment. I've found new life." She once was lost but now she is found.

If you have a trauma similar to Erin's, please don't let it linger another day. God's desire is for wholeness and strength. He will walk with you through your pain. Erin made an important decision to seek help. You can't wish away these issues.

- By age 18, 1 out of 4 young women are sexually abused.[1]
- By age 18, 1 out of 8 young men are sexually abused.[2]

If you have ever been abused and you have not thoroughly talked about it, then please do so with a trusted adult counselor, pastor, youth worker or church leader today. If you have no one with whom to talk, then call one of these two numbers.

- Sexual Abuse Help Line: 1-800-4-A-CHILD (24-hours, toll-free)
- National Youth Crisis Hotline of Youth Development International (YDI): 1-800-HIT-HOME

FURTHER FATHOM

- Take a moment to pray for people in your school, club, family and community who have been abused.

POWERFUL PRAISE

I come to you, LORD, for protection; never let me be defeated. You are a righteous God; save me, I pray! Hear me! Save me now! Be my refuge to protect me; my defense to save me. You are my refuge and defense; guide me and lead me as you have promised. Keep me safe from the trap that has been set for me; shelter me from danger. I place myself in your care. You will save me, LORD; you are a faithful God.

PSALM 31:1-5

RAPID RECAP

- Many young people are sexually abused.
- There is help. God will fill the void and take away the hurt.

GREAT JOY

*I have told you this so that my joy may be in you and that
your joy may be complete.*

JOHN 15:11

Today we need to laugh. Through the years, there have been some funny church-bulletin bloopers. Here are a few of my personal favorites:

- This afternoon, there will be a meeting in the north and south ends of the church and children will be christened at both ends.
- Tuesday at 7:00 P.M. there will be an invitation to an ice-cream social. All ladies giving milk, please come early.
- Wednesday, the Ladies Literary Society will meet and Mrs. Lacey will sing, "Put Me in My Little Bed" accompanied by the Reverend.
- This Sunday, being Easter, we will ask Mrs. Daly to come forward and lay an egg on the altar.[1]

The Graduate School of Education at Northern Illinois University, DeKalb, collected a number of excuses parents gave to school officials when their son or daughter missed classes. Here are some of them, with their grammar and spelling left intact:

- Please excuse John for being absent January 28, 29, 30, 32 and 33.
- John has been absent because he has two teeth taken out of his face.
- My son is under the doctor's care and should not take PE. Please execute him.
- Please excuse Joey on Friday. He had loose vowels.[2]

Of course we understood what these parents meant to say about their kids' sicknesses and problems but it didn't come out just right.

Far too many people think God is the great killjoy. I have a feeling that when He saw those bloopers, He and some of His angels had a belly laugh. Joy and laughter come from God. Take a moment today to celebrate His presence in your life.

I have heard it put this way: If Christians have really been redeemed, someone should remind them to tell their face. Smile! God loves you! "The joy of the LORD is your strength" (Neh. 8:10).

FURTHER FATHOMS

- List several reasons why you can be filled with joy.
- Can you find any situation in which you might see that God really does have a sense of humor?

POWERFUL PRAISE

The LORD is great and is to be highly praised in the city of our God, on his sacred hill. Zion, the mountain of God, is high and beautiful; the city of the great

king brings joy to all the world. God has shown that there is
safety with him inside the fortresses of the city.

PSALM 48:1-3

RAPID RECAP

- God has a sense of humor
- It is good to be filled with joy and laughter.

GOD PROVIDES

Ask and it will be given to you; seek and you will find; knock and the door will be opened to you. For everyone who asks receives; he who seeks finds; and to him who knocks, the doors will be opened. Which of you, if his son asks for bread, will give him a stone? Or if he asks for a fish, will give him a snake? If you, then, though you are evil, know how to give good gifts to your children, how much more will your Father in heaven give good gifts to those who ask him!

MATTHEW 7:7-11

God cares for you. He wants the best for you. He always has your best interest in mind. Because He is your loving heavenly Father you must tell him your needs constantly. He wants to provide abundant life and abundant blessings for you.

George Muller was a man of great faith in our God as a provider for the children in his orphanage in England, Ashley Downs. One day, things looked bleak at the orphanage. It was time for breakfast, but there was no food. A small girl, whose father was a close friend of Muller, was visiting Ashley Downs. Muller took her hand and said, "Come and see what our Father will do." In the dining room, long tables were set with empty plates and empty mugs. There was no food in the kitchen, and no money in the orphanage's account. Muller prayed, "Dear Father, we thank Thee for what Thou art going to give us to eat." Immediately, they heard a knock at the door. When Muller opened it, there stood the local baker. "Mr. Muller," he said, "Last night I could not sleep. Somehow I knew that you would need bread this morning. I got up and baked three batches for you. I will bring it in." Muller thanked him and gave praise to God. Soon, a second knock was heard. It was the milkman. His cart had broken down in front of the orphanage. He said he would like to give the children the milk so that he could empty the cart and repair it.[1]

There's a word that comes to my mind after reading that incredible story. It's not necessarily a spiritual word—but it's the word I bet was also on the minds of the hungry children that day: "Wow!" What else can you do but take a moment to thank God for all his provisions?

FURTHER FATHOMS

- Why is this story so inspiring?
- Take a few minutes and list the many ways God has provided for you this past week (even if you took most of it for granted).

POWERFUL PRAISE

Clap your hands for joy, all peoples! Praise God with loud songs! The LORD, the Most High, is to be feared; he is a great king, ruling over all the world. He gave us victory over the peoples; he made us rule over the nations. He chose for us the land where we live, the proud possession of his people, whom he loves. God goes up to his throne. There are shouts of joy and the blast of trumpets, as the LORD goes up. Sing praise to God; sing praise to our king! God is king over all the world; praise him with songs! God sits on his sacred throne; he rules over the nations. The rulers of the nations assemble with the people of the God of Abraham. More powerful than all armies is he; he rules supreme.

PSALM 47

Rapid Recap

- God is our provider.
- Even when the circumstances look bleak, He will come through.

BIG POWER

But you will receive power when the Holy Spirit comes on you;
and you will be my witnesses in Jerusalem, and in all Judea
and Samaria, and to the ends of the earth.

ACTS 1:8

At 5:04 P.M. on October 17, 1989, I was speaking to a group of youth workers at a convention in San Francisco. It had been a great day; many of us had plans to watch the World Series that night (being played down the street from the hotel where I was speaking and staying). But our plans changed abruptly. The room began to shake; the chandeliers moved back and forth. I quit speaking and there was a deafening silence. Everyone watched and waited. And then it hit: The Big One.

We all ran outside. People screamed, some cried. Most of us just looked around in awe at the incredible power of this quake. We watched the hotel across the street lose the entire front of the building. Water shot out of pipes. It was devastating and frightening.

Later we heard the news that all of the Bay Area was paralyzed.

• 67 people had been killed.
• 6 billion dollars of damage had been done to property.
• 12,000 people were left homeless.[1]

The magnitude 7.1 earthquake lasted only 15 seconds but its

force will forever be ingrained on my life. When I think about this experience, the word that comes to my mind is "power." The raw power of the earth shaking forced millions of people to stop and adjust their lives.

Why does it take an earthquake or another powerful event to get our attention when in reality we have the awesome power of God available to us through His Holy Spirit?

You can tap into the power of God by yielding to His Holy Spirit. If the earth stores up ferocious power for destruction, imagine God's power to do good in the world He created.

FURTHER FATHOMS

- If you could draw upon God's power today, what would you ask Him to do?
- Take a moment to pray and ask the Holy Spirit to fill and empower you.

POWERFUL PRAISE

Praise the LORD, you heavenly beings; praise his glory and power. Praise the LORD's glorious name; bow down before the Holy One when he appears. The voice of the LORD is heard on the seas; the glorious God thunders, and his voice echoes over the ocean. The voice of the LORD is heard in all its might and majesty.

PSALM 29:1–4

RAPID RECAP

- God's power is available to us through His Holy Spirit.
- God's power is greater than any earthly power.

WEEK 4

ORDINARY PEOPLE DOING EXTRAORDINARY THINGS

Being confident of this, that he who began a good work in you will carry it on to completion until the day of Christ Jesus.

PHILIPPIANS 1:6

FAITH IS

Now faith is being sure of what we hope for and certain of what we do not see. And without faith it is impossible to please God, because anyone who comes to him must believe that he exists and that he rewards those who earnestly seek him.

HEBREWS 11:1,6

What are you doing right now that you could not do without the help of our supernatural God? When we think of the word faith, we often think of the most incredible miracles we have ever heard about. I don't know about you but I believe in those kinds of miracles of faith. Sometimes God chooses to heal a person with cancer or whatever physical problem he or she has. In fact, I have even heard of God giving a van supernatural extra gas mileage when a group of people were smuggling Bibles into a country where God's Word was forbidden. There are other times when people have just as much faith but God chooses not to heal or to do a miracle.

Faith also describes what ordinary people have when they do extraordinary things with their lives.

Faith is Bob Wieland walking across America on his hands because he has no feet! Faith is missionary Tammy Fong Heilemann moving from California to Kompong Cham, Cambodia, so that she can help young girls escape the quagmire of prostitution and turn their lives around. Faith is Rebecca St. James declaring before the world that she will remain sexually abstinent until she is married.

Faith is Ted choosing not to cheat on his geometry exam. Faith is 18-year-old Rachel deciding not to abort her baby. Faith is Mitch telling his Jewish parents that he has accepted Jesus as Messiah.

Faith is not doing something when everyone else is doing it or doing something even when no one else is doing it. It's not getting drunk even though you are in college and want to be accepted in the fraternity. It's walking away from riches because God's call on your life is to be a missionary. It's waiting for the right man to marry even though your biological clock is ticking. Faith is placing all that you are, all that you can be and all that you do into the hands of God.

Faith is doing something you could not do or being someone who you could not be without the help of our supernatural God.

What are you doing in faith right now? Take a moment and ask God to make you an ordinary person doing extraordinary things for Him.

FURTHER FATHOMS

- How does Hebrews 11:1,6 relate to your life?
- What areas of your life could use a real faith-lift?

POWERFUL PRAISE

LORD, I have come to you for protection; never let me be defeated! Because you are righteous, help me and rescue me. Listen to me and save me! Be my secure shelter and a strong fortress to protect me; you are my refuge and defense. My God, rescue me from wicked people, from the power of cruel and evil people. Sovereign LORD, I put my hope in you; I have trusted in you since I was young.

I have relied on you all my life; you have protected me since the day I was born.
I will always praise you. My life has been an example to many, because you have
been my strong defender. All day long I praise you and proclaim your glory.

PSALM 71:1-8

RAPID RECAP

- Our supernatural God is ready to help us.
- Faith is ordinary people doing extraordinary acts with God's help.

GIVING TO OTHERS

This is how we know what love is: Jesus Christ laid down his life for us. And we ought to lay down our lives for our brothers. If anyone has material possessions and sees his brother in need but has no pity on him, how can the love of God be in him? Dear children, let us not love with words or tongue but with actions and in truth.

1 JOHN 3:16-18

A little boy was told by his doctor that he could save his sister's life by giving her some blood. The six-year-old girl was near death, a victim of a disease from which the boy had made a marvelous recovery two years earlier. Her only chance for restoration was a blood transfusion from someone who had previously conquered the illness. Since the two children had the same rare blood type, the boy was the ideal donor.

"Johnny, would you like to give your blood for Mary?" the doctor asked. The boy hesitated. His lower lip started to tremble. Then he smiled and said, "Sure, Doc. I'll give my blood for my sister."

Soon the two children were wheeled into the operating room—Mary, pale and thin; Johnny, robust and the picture of health. Neither spoke, but when their eyes met, Johnny grinned.

As his blood siphoned into Mary's veins, one could almost see new life come into her tired body. The ordeal was almost over when Johnny's brave little voice broke the silence, "Say, Doc, when do I die?"

It was only then that the doctor realized what the moment of hesitation, the trembling of the lip, had meant earlier. Little Johnny actually thought that in giving his blood to his sister he was giving up his life! And in that brief moment, he had made his sacrificial decision! Jesus Christ died for you and me. God offered us not only great love but also a great example.

FURTHER FATHOMS

- Read John 15:13. How does this Scripture apply to this incredible story of Johnny and his sister? Where is Jesus in this story?
- How can you apply this type of sacrificial giving to your own life?

POWERFUL PRAISE

Happy are those who are concerned for the poor; the LORD will help them when they are in trouble. The LORD will protect them and preserve their lives; he will make them happy in the land; he will not abandon them to the power of their enemies. The LORD will help them when they are sick and will restore them to health. You will help me, because I do what is right; you will keep me in your presence forever. Praise the LORD, the God of Israel! Praise him now and forever! Amen! Amen!

PSALM 41:1-3,12-13

RAPID RECAP

- Jesus gave His life so that we might live.
- We are likewise to make sacrifices for others.

EXTRAORDINARY LOVE

*On one occasion an expert in the law stood up to test Jesus. "Teacher," he
asked, "what must I do to inherit eternal life?" "What is written in the
Law?" he replied. "How do you read it?" He answered: "'Love the LORD
your God with all your heart and with all your soul and with all your
strength and with all your mind'; and, 'Love your neighbor as yourself.'"
"You have answered correctly," Jesus replied. "Do this and you will live."
But he wanted to justify himself, so he asked Jesus, "And who is my neighbor?" In reply Jesus said: "A man was going down from Jerusalem to
Jericho, when he fell into the hands of robbers. They stripped him of his
clothes, beat him and went away, leaving him half dead. A priest happened to be going down the same road, and when he saw the man, he
passed by on the other side. So too, a Levite, when he came to the place
and saw him, passed by on the other side. But a Samaritan, as he traveled, came where the man was; and when he saw him, he took pity on
him. He went to him and bandaged his wounds, pouring on oil and wine.
Then he put the man on his own donkey, took him to an inn and took
care of him. The next day he took out two silver coins and gave them to
the innkeeper. 'Look after him,' he said, 'and when I return I will reim-
burse you for any extra expense you may have.' Which of these three do
you think was a neighbor to the man who fell into the hands of robbers?"
The expert in the law replied, "The one who had mercy on him." Jesus
told him, "Go and do likewise."*

LUKE 10:25-37

Today's Scripture is insightful, powerful and, to be perfectly honest, very challenging. Let's look at the main characters.

- The traveler: Here's a nice guy minding his own business when he gets attacked by the robbers. He has everything stolen, is beaten and is left for dead. We definitely meet a man in need of help.
- The priest: This person looked holy and spiritual. He knew the Bible, did the right kinds of things, said all the right stuff, but it was all for show. On the outside he appeared religious, but on the inside he was nothing but a hypocrite. Jesus described this as "whitewashed tombs, which look beautiful on the outside but on the inside are full of dead men's bones and everything unclean" (Matt. 23:27). (You can check out Matthew 23 for what Jesus thinks of hypocrites. Believe me, it's not a pleasant chapter!)
- The Levite: Here's a person who is basically self-centered. I really believe the Levite (he was not called a Levite because he wore Levi's!) had a sincere heart for God but simply never got around to living for God. He meant well but his actions spoke louder than his words. Ultimately, he was too busy to care for the needy traveler and thought someone else would do it. (Ouch! I can relate to this guy too often in my life.)
- The Samaritan: Samaritans were not popular with Jews. In fact, Jews didn't socialize or even speak to Samaritans. Yet this Samaritan had a heart for God. He noticed the needy traveler and responded with his time and his money. The Samaritan was an ordinary person doing an extraordinary act of love. Oh, that we may

become more like this Samaritan and learn a lesson from this story.

· Which kind of neighbor are you?

FURTHER FATHOMS

· What is the central theme of this story in the Bible?
· What can you do this week to put this lesson into action steps for your life?

POWERFUL PRAISE

As high as the sky is above the earth, so great is his love for those who honor him. As far as the east is from the west, so far does he remove our sins from us. As a father is kind to his children, so the LORD is kind to those who honor him.

PSALM 103:11-13

RAPID RECAP

· God uses ordinary people.
· He may call upon us to help someone in need.

GOD KNOWS WHAT HE IS DOING!

*And we know that in all things God works for the good of those who love him,
who have been called according to his purpose.*

ROMANS 8:28

Os Hillman tells a story about how God's purpose can prevail over our plans. From a very young age, Samuel Morse had a strong desire to be an artist. He had talent and was able to master his craft. Finally, the day came when he was able to sell some of his work. But the fulfillment of his dream was short-lived. It was difficult to make a living as an artist, and he suffered a series of personal setbacks.

Heartbroken, Samuel went to Europe to mull over his situation. On his return trip—aboard a ship crossing the Atlantic—Samuel heard about advances in electromagnetism. "If the presence of electricity can be made visible in any part of the circuit, I see no reason why intelligence may not be transmitted by electricity." [1]

Samuel worked hard. Acting on what he had learned on the ship, he invented the telegraph and developed Morse Code. Eventually, his projects received needed funding. In hindsight,

Samuel said, "The only gleam of hope, and I cannot underrate it, is from confidence in God. When I look upward it calms any apprehension for the future, and I seem to hear a voice saying: 'If I clothe the lilies of the field, shall I not also clothe you?' Here is my strong confidence, and I will wait patiently for the direction of Providence."[2]

Without Samuel Morse's initial inventions, today we might not have faxes, e-mail or the Internet. God's plans are not always our plans, for His plans often carry an even greater purpose. "The LORD works out everything for His own ends—even the wicked for a day of disaster" (Prov. 16:4).

FURTHER FATHOMS

- What plans do you have that must continually be given over to God?
- Why is it difficult to put our plans and trust in God even when we read Scriptures such as Romans 8:28?

POWERFUL PRAISE

How I love you, LORD! You are my defender. The LORD is my protector; he is my strong fortress. My God is my protection, and with him I am safe. He protects me like a shield; he defends me and keeps me safe. I call to the LORD, and he saves me from my enemies. Praise the LORD!

PSALM 18:1-3

RAPID RECAP

- God's plans are not always our plans.
- God always has a plan with a greater purpose and lots of fruit.

A GREAT STORY

Therefore go and make disciples of all nations, baptizing them in the
name of the Father and of the Son and of the Holy Spirit,
and teaching them to obey everything I have commanded you.
And surely I am with you always, to the very end of the age.

MATTHEW 28:19-20

In 1858, Edward Kimbell, a Sunday school teacher, prayed with one of his students, a shoe salesman. The salesman, Dwight L. Moody, accepted Christ as his Savior and went on to became a great evangelist.[1] In 1879, Moody was sharing the good news of Jesus and a young man, F. B. Meyer, met Christ; this young man became zealous for preaching the good news. While preaching on an American college campus, F. B. Meyer brought a student, J. Wilbur Chapman, to Christ. Chapman later employed a former baseball player, Billy Sunday, to do evangelistic work.

Billy Sunday was one of the greatest Christian preachers and evangelists in the early 1900s. Once, after Billy Sunday preached in Charlotte, North Carolina, a group of local businessmen became so enthusiastic, they decided to bring another man, Mordecai Ham, to preach. During Ham's revival meeting, a young man, Billy Graham, yielded his life to Christ. Billy Graham has since preached to more people in person than any other person in history. Only God can count how many people have been reached by people who were saved at Graham's meetings.

It all started with a faithful Sunday school teacher, Edward Kimbell. Few people will ever know his name but look at how many people this one man's witness has affected.

The world has yet to see what one man or woman can do for Christ if they are *completely* yielded to Him. Will you be a person such as Edward Kimbell who was faithful in sharing the good news of Jesus? You never know what can happen. There could be another Dwight Moody, Billy Sunday or Billy Graham out there waiting to be converted.

Here's what the Scripture declares about those who share the good news: "How beautiful on the mountains are the feet of those who bring good news, who proclaim peace, who bring good tidings, who proclaim salvation, who say to Zion, 'Your God reigns!'" (Isa. 52:7).

FURTHER FATHOMS

- How does Isaiah 52:7 inspire you?
- Think of three people who are not Christians. Pray for them and then look for opportunities to share the good news with them in the next month.

POWERFUL PRAISE

Sing a new song to the LORD; he has done wonderful things! By his own power and holy strength he has won the victory. The LORD announced his victory; he made his saving power known to the nations. He kept his promise to the people of Israel with loyalty and constant love for them. All people everywhere have seen the victory of our God. Sing for joy to the LORD, all the earth; praise him with songs and shouts of joy!

PSALM 98:1-4

Rapid Recap

- One person can make a difference.
- We should be looking for opportunities to share the good news.

GOD CAN USE YOU

As Jesus was getting into the boat, the man who had been demon-possessed begged to go with him. Jesus did not let him, but said, "Go home to your family and tell them how much the LORD has done for you, and how he has had mercy on you." So the man went away and began to tell in the Decapolis how much Jesus had done for him. And all the people were amazed.

MARK 5:18-20

If you want to read a great Bible story, take a moment to ponder Mark 5:1-20. It shows how Jesus used a crazy person to spread the word of God.

Imagine for a moment that this conversation took place one day when Jesus and His disciples were out on the Sea of Galilee. They were headed in a southeasterly direction out of Capernaum. The disciples asked Jesus where they were heading and for what purpose. Jesus answered, "Oh, we're heading over toward the area of the ten Greek cities, the Decapolis."

The disciples asked, "What for?"

He replied, "We're going to get the message of the Kingdom out throughout that entire region."

"My," Peter said. "That's quite a task. How many weeks will we be there? I didn't really come prepared."

"You don't understand," said Jesus. "We'll just be there a few hours, maybe the better part of the day."

"Well, frankly, LORD, I'm totally confused. How in the world can we get the message out in such a short time?" asked another.

"Oh, I've got it all figured out," said Jesus. "I've got a man picked out over there. We'll be meeting him a bit after we land. He's going to spread the word."

"Well," said Peter, "now I understand. Is it anyone we know?"

"No, you've never met this fellow before."

"He must be quite a guy if he's going to take on this territory all by himself. He must have some charisma or training. I'll bet he's one of those sharp, well-educated young Pharisees who were converted down at the seminary in Jerusalem during our last visit there! Right?" someone asked.

"No," Jesus said. "Actually, he hasn't had any training at all. And frankly, he hasn't gone to school much either. As a matter of fact, mostly he has just been hanging around the cemetery lately."

"The cemetery? What is he, a funeral director? Or a grave digger? What does he do at the cemetery?" a disciple demanded.

"Well, mainly he runs around breaking chains, cutting himself and banging his head on the stone markers. As a matter of fact, right now he's full of the devil and running around half nuts."

Do you get the idea? Only God knows the power and potential within each one of us. Isn't it amazing that He uses ordinary people like you and me to accomplish His plans? If God can use a demon-possessed man to spread the word (see Mark 5:20), then He can surely use us as well. What about you? Will you allow yourself to be an ordinary person whom God uses to do extraordinary things?

FURTHER FATHOMS

- Why do you think Jesus used regular people—or even very needy people, as opposed to the most talented people of His day—to further God's kingdom?
- How can this story be meaningful in your life?

POWERFUL PRAISE

Give thanks to the LORD, because he is good; his love is eternal. Give thanks to the greatest of all gods; his love is eternal. Give thanks to the mightiest of all lords; his love is eternal. He alone performs great miracles; his love is eternal. By his wisdom he made the heavens; his love is eternal; he built the earth on the deep waters; his love is eternal. He made the sun and the moon; his love is eternal; the sun to rule over the day; his love is eternal; the moon and stars to rule over the night; his love is eternal.

PSALM 136:1-9

RAPID RECAP

- There is power and potential within each of us.
- God decides who is best to accomplish each task.

THE POWER OF AFFIRMATION

If anyone considers himself religious and yet does not keep a tight rein on his tongue, he deceives himself and his religion is worthless.

JAMES 1:26

Cheryl Prewitt Salem was Miss America in 1980. Cheryl is a beautiful person on the outside but moreover her inner beauty radiates God's love in her life. When she was four years old she often hung around her father's small country store. Almost daily the milkman would visit, and she would follow him around as he lined the display cases with shiny bottles of milk. He always greeted her the same way: "How's my little Miss America?" At first she giggled, but by about age 11 she became very comfortable with this idea of becoming Miss America. Before long it was her childhood fantasy and teenage dream. It became a prayer and a solid goal.

Later she did become Miss America. She traveled the world spreading goodwill and, because Cheryl is a deeply committed Christian, the gospel of Jesus Christ.

It all started because God used a milkman to speak a word to this young and impressionable mind. It was embedded in her subconscious. Her prayer became a reality.

The tongue has the power of life and death, and those who love it will eat its fruit (Prov. 18:21).

Can God use your tongue to offer an affirming word to someone?

FURTHER FATHOMS

- Is there someone in your life to affirm today? Of course there is! Who is it and how will you affirm him or her?
- Read James 3:310. What is the lesson from this section of Scripture?

POWERFUL PRAISE

May my words and my thoughts be acceptable to you,
O LORD, my refuge and my redeemer!

PSALM 19:14

RAPID RECAP

- Our words are powerful.
- Affirming words can shape a person's life.

WEEK 5

CHANGING THE
WAY YOU THINK

*Do not be anxious about anything, but in everything, by prayer and petition, with
thanksgiving, present your requests to God. And the peace of God, which transcends all understanding, will guard your hearts and your minds in Christ Jesus.*

PHILIPPIANS 4:6-7

GETTING YOUR PRIORITIES STRAIGHT

*And whatever you do, whether in word or deed, do it all in the name of the
LORD Jesus, giving thanks to God the Father through him.*

COLOSSIANS 3:17

Amber Thomason punched her alarm clock off at 7:01 A.M.
and rolled out of bed. She had meant to get up earlier to have her
quiet time with God but last night she had gone to bed late—
there had been dinner, homework, a phone call and the TV. In
addition, she had dilly-dallied with her makeup and her hair
before finally crashing into bed. She had meant to pray then but
simply had forgotten. At 7:02 A.M., she quickly started her morning routine, which included clothes, teeth, hair, more hair, a
quick bite and a glance at her homework. Rush, rush, hurry,
hurry. She picked up Janine on the way to school, had a great
talk about Tyler, complained about Mr. Shelton's class, and gos-
siped just a little about Marissa and Brandon.

School was a blur. Classes were OK. It was almost summer-
time. *Then,* Amber told herself, *I will really start spending time with
God.* In Mr. Shelton's class, everyone talked about God but they

didn't talk to God. She remembered that at youth group Mr. Bodnar invited people to go on another mission trip to an Indian reservation. *One of these days,* Amber told herself, *I would really like to go, but not this time.* She was just too busy.

After school Amber was swamped. At dinner with half the Thomason family present, her mom asked her if she was going to youth group tonight. She definitely wanted to go but once again her homework wasn't done. Instead of going to the youth group meeting, Amber crammed for a math test. Her brother turned on the TV and her sister played the latest ZoeGirl tape. Amber stopped to listen and watch. After a few phone calls and two hours of watching TV with her books on her lap, she headed for bed. She didn't even remove her eye mascara. Amber stopped for a moment and looked at the devotional on the table by her bed. She was way too tired. Maybe tomorrow she would wake up early.

She woke to the alarm at 7:01 A.M. and rolled out of bed. She had meant to get up earlier and do that devotional but—*This summer,* Amber told herself, *I will get my priorities straight.* Of course, that is what she had said last summer, too.

Can you relate to Amber's schedule and even her desire to spend time with God? Amber means well, she just never gets around to putting her priorities in order. What if she made a three-month commitment to God to spend a few minutes a day with Him? Does that seem too difficult? How about you? What if you made a three-month commitment to God to spend 10 minutes a day with Him? Can you do that? Do you have the time? Is it worth the energy?

Today, make a commitment to give God 10 minutes a day for the next three months. These devotionals can assist you in your times with God. It is a challenge from me to you. Here's my guarantee: If you spend 10 minutes a day with God on a regular basis for three months, you won't be the same person you were when you started. OK, it's a challenge, right? Go for it. You'll be glad you did.

FURTHER FATHOMS

- Will you make a commitment today to give God 10 minutes each day for the next three months?
- Read Joshua 1:8. How might the scriptural promise in this passage motivate you?

POWERFUL PRAISE

Happy are those whose lives are faultless, who live according to the law of the LORD. Happy are those who follow his commands, who obey him with all their heart. They never do wrong; they walk in the LORD's ways. How can young people keep their lives pure? By obeying your commands. With all my heart I try to serve you; keep me from disobeying your commandments. I keep your law in my heart, so that I will not sin against you.

PSALM 119:1-3,9-11

RAPID RECAP

- We all need to get our priorities straight.
- Spending time with God should be our greatest priority.

ATTITUDE AND CIRCUMSTANCE

I have learned to be content whatever the circumstances. I know what it is to be in need, and I know what it is to have plenty. I have learned the secret of being content in any and every situation, whether well fed or hungry, whether living in plenty or in want. I can do everything through him who gives me strength.

PHILIPPIANS 4:11-13

I enjoy the story of the little boy who was talking to himself as he strutted through the backyard, baseball cap in place, toting a ball and a bat. He was overheard to say, "I'm the greatest hitter in the world." Then he tossed the ball into the air, swung at it and missed. "Strike one." Undaunted he picked up the ball, said to himself, "I'm the greatest baseball hitter ever," threw the ball into the air and swung at the ball a second time. Again he missed. "Strike two!" He paused a moment to examine his bat and ball carefully. "I'm the greatest hitter who ever lived," he exclaimed. Then a third time he threw the ball into the air, swung the bat hard, and missed yet again. He cried out, "Wow! Strike three. What a pitcher! I'm the greatest pitcher in the world!"

His circumstances hadn't changed but his attitude had changed, and that makes all the difference in the world. What difficulties are you facing right now? Is there really something that can change it? If you can do something about it, great, don't wait another day. But if you can't change the circumstances, then change your attitude—that will make all the difference in the world.

FURTHER FATHOMS

- What circumstances in your life do you need to turn over to God?
- What makes it difficult to apply the principles of today's lesson in your life?

POWERFUL PRAISE

As a deer longs for a stream of cool water, so I long for you, O God. I thirst for you, the living God. When can I go and worship in your presence? Day and night I cry, and tears are my only food; all the time my enemies ask me, "Where is your God?" My heart breaks when I remember the past, when I went with the crowds to the house of God and led them as they walked along, a happy crowd, singing and shouting praise to God. Why am I so sad? Why am I so troubled? I will put my hope in God, and once again I will praise him, my savior and my God. Here in exile my heart is breaking, and so I turn my thoughts to him.

PSALM 42:1-6

RAPID RECAP

- Our attitude affects how we see our situation.
- If we cannot change our circumstances, at least we can change our attitude.

MAKING PEOPLE
BRAND NEW

And let us consider how we may spur one another on toward love and good deeds.
Let us not give up meeting together, as some are in the habit of doing, but let us
encourage one another—and all the more as you see the Day approaching.

HEBREWS 10:24-25

One of my favorite musicals is *Man of La Mancha*. In this story, we meet a loony Spanish gentleman, Don Quixote, who thinks he is an honored knight, when in fact he is nothing of the sort. Don Quixote meets a lowly prostitute, Aldonza. He doesn't know she is a prostitute; he thinks she is an elegant Spanish lady, a queen. Yet Don Quixote slowly changes the entire self-concept of this prostitute by constantly, unconditionally affirming her. What is amazing about the story is that when she begins to see herself differently, she begins to act differently. He even gives her a new name, Dulcinea, so that she will forever be reminded of her new identity and her potential. She becomes a brand-new person.[1]

Who is the Aldonza in your life? To whom can you offer positive encouragement? Who can you believe in even when he or she doesn't believe in himself or herself? In order to affirm a person's potential, you may have to look at that person with the eyes of faith and treat him or her in terms of his or her potential, not his or her behavior.

Goethe, a famous philosopher, put it this way:

Treat a man as he is, and he will remain as he is; treat a man as he can be and should be and he will become as he can be and should be.[2]

Again I ask, who is the Aldonza in your life? Who do you know who can become a Dulcinea? Today is the day to believe in him or her—and give him or her the gift of affirmation.

FURTHER FATHOMS

- Read Ephesians 2:10. How does this verse apply to today's reading?
- Write three specific goals to help affirm the Aldonza in your life.

POWERFUL PRAISE

Give thanks to the LORD, because he is good, and his love is eternal. Let the people of Israel say, "His love is eternal." Let the priests of God say, "His love is eternal." Let all who worship him say, "His love is eternal."

PSALM 118:1-4

RAPID RECAP

- Our words are powerful.
- Affirmation can transform a person's self-image and then his or her actions.

HOLD THAT CRITICISM

Do not judge, or you too will be judged. For in the same way you judge others, you will be judged, and with the measure you use, it will be measured to you.

MATTHEW 7:1-2

Here is a huge challenge: Go on a fast from criticism. Today, your assignment is not to criticize anybody about anything. Just for 24 hours, even if you have a legitimate criticism, don't offer it. Most of us are far too critical. We offer lots of grumbling and complaining about issues that frankly don't make much difference. All of the criticism has a very negative result. Critical people are often unhappy people. The act of criticizing drains positive energy from our lives.

I once heard it put it this way:

A critical spirit focuses us on ourselves and makes us unhappy. We lose perspective and humor.

A critical spirit blocks the positive creative thoughts God longs to give us.

A critical spirit can prevent good relationships between individuals and often produces retaliatory criticalness.

Criticalness blocks the work of the Spirit of God: love, goodwill and mercy.

Whenever we see something genuinely wrong in another person's behavior, rather than criticize him or her directly, or far worse, gripe about him behind his back, we should ask the spirit of God to do the correction needed.[1]

"Do everything without complaining or arguing" (Phil. 2:14). This means that if you're driving today and someone cuts you off—do not complain. If you get disconnected from your cell-phone call—do not complain. If someone spills split-pea soup on your best shirt—do not complain. Understand and accept, rather than fume and whine. A wise friend once told me that we never know enough about a situation to be truly angry. Think about it.

I have the feeling that you are going to have a very good day!

FURTHER FATHOMS

- Read and memorize Philippians 2:14.
- What specific areas of a critical spirit can you work on today—and this week?

POWERFUL PRAISE

Honor the LORD, all his people; those who obey him have all they need. Even lions go hungry for lack of food, but those who obey the LORD lack nothing good. Come, my young friends, and listen to me, and I will teach you to honor the LORD. Would you like to enjoy life? Do you want long life and happiness? Then keep from speak-

ing evil and from telling lies. Turn away from evil and do good; strive for peace with all your heart. The LORD watches over the righteous and listens to their cries.

PSALM 34:9-15

RAPID RECAP

- Critical people are unhappy people.
- We should do everything without complaining or grumbling.

LIVING BEYOND THE CIRCUMSTANCE

Do not be anxious about anything, but in everything, by prayer and petition, with thanksgiving, present your requests to God. And the peace of God, which transcends all understanding, will guard your hearts and your minds in Christ Jesus.

PHILIPPIANS 4:6-7

Kathleen's parents are getting a divorce. Matt's mom is an alcoholic. Lindsey's dad was fired from his job. Tony didn't make the cut on the basketball team. Jana has never had a date. And Jared had to have his third operation in three years. Each of these people is living under some pretty crummy circumstances. Each one of them wishes that his or her problem would disappear. Each has prayed about his or her issue and yet the problem won't go away.

What are your problems? No doubt, like all of us, you, too, have issues that make your life less than perfect.

Your circumstances may never change but your attitude can change; when it does, it makes all the difference in the world. If you can do something about your problems, then by all means make a wise decision. If you can get rid of them, do it. However, there are some problems you have no control over. These are the problems that can teach you a lesson to live beyond your circumstances.

Terry Fox ran a marathon every day for 143 days to raise money for cancer research until his own cancer forced him to stop. He ran on one leg; the other leg had been amputated because of cancer.[1]

Rachel was beaten by her mother and abused by her father. Although life wasn't easy, she decided to get help. Her past couldn't change, so she worked through her attitude. Today she helps other teenagers from abused homes find a meaningful life.

What about you? Do you need a dose of attitude change today? With God's help you can overcome most any problem. Don't wait another day for an attitude adjustment. Learn to be thankful even in the midst of difficult circumstances. The result is "the peace of God, which transcends all understanding" (Phil. 4:7).

FURTHER FATHOMS

- What steps can you take in your own life to live beyond your circumstances?
- What is the formula found in Philippians 4:6-7 that will guarantee you peace?

POWERFUL PRAISE

I wait patiently for God to save me; I depend on him alone. He alone protects and saves me; he is my defender, and I shall never be defeated. I depend on God alone; I put my hope in him. He alone protects and saves me; he is my defender, and I shall never be defeated. My salvation and honor depend on God; he is my strong protector; he is my shelter.

PSALM 62:1-2,5-8

RAPID RECAP

- We all have circumstances in our lives that are beyond our control.
- A positive attitude will help us overcome negative circumstances.

LIVING IN THE FAST LANE

The LORD will fight for you; you need only to be still.

EXODUS 14:14

Far too many people live in crisis-living mode. This lifestyle is when you spend most every waking moment of almost every day trying to figure how to keep all your plates spinning and how to juggle all the balls in the air. In crisis mode you keep running, even on empty. You keep running faster and faster, moving from project to project, deadline to deadline at breakneck speed. You juggle school, jobs, friends, church, lessons and homework.

Usually people who live this kind of lifestyle eventually crash. Their plates fall and they have to pick up the pieces of their lives.

I keep these important words close to my heart. There is a lot of wisdom and prevention in them:

Slow me down, LORD.
Ease the pounding of my heart by the quieting of my
    mind.
Steady my hurried pace with a vision of the eternal
    reach of time.

Give me, amid the confusion of the day, the calmness
of the everlasting hills.

Break the tensions of my nerves and muscles with the
soothing music of the singing streams that live in my
memory.
Teach me the art of taking minute vacations—of slow-
ing down to look at a flower, to chat with a friend, to
pat a dog, to smile at a child, to read a few lines from
a good book.

Slow me down, LORD, and inspire me to send my roots
deep into the soil of life's enduring values, that I may
grow toward my greater destiny.
Remind me each day that the race is not always to the
swift; that there is more to life than increasing its
speed.
Let me look upward to the towering oak and know that
it grew great and strong because it grew slowly and
well.[1]

I know this is an old cliché, but think about it: When was the
last time you stopped to smell the flowers? Slow down and learn
to enjoy the simple things in life.

FURTHER FATHOMS

- What is the message in today's devotional for you?
- A friend of mine once told me, "If the devil can't make
you bad, then he will make you busy." What do you
think that statement means?

POWERFUL PRAISE

Be patient and wait for the LORD to act; don't be worried about those who prosper or those who succeed in their evil plans. Don't give in to worry or anger, it only leads to trouble. Those who trust in the LORD will possess the land, but the wicked will be driven out. Soon the wicked will disappear; you may look for them, but you won't find them; but the humble will possess the land and enjoy prosperity and peace.

PSALM 37:7-11

RAPID RECAP

- Too many people live in crisis mode.
- Stop and smell the flowers.

CHECKING YOUR ATTITUDE

Consider it pure joy, my brothers, whenever you face trials of many kinds, because you know that the testing of your faith develops perseverance. Perseverance must finish its work so that you may be mature and complete, not lacking anything.

JAMES 1:2-4

A confederate soldier in the midst of some very trying circumstances wrote the words below. I don't know who he was or where he learned this incredible principle of life, but I offer it to you today as one of the secrets of a fulfilled life. I read this poem often and I call it my attitude check.

> I asked God for strength that I might achieve. I was
>   made weak that I might learn humbly to obey.
> I asked God for health that I might do greater things.
>   I was given infirmity that I might do better things.
> I asked for riches that I might be happy. I was given
>   poverty that I might be wise.
> I asked for power that I might have the praise of men.
>   I was given weakness that I might feel the need of God.
> I asked for all things that I might enjoy life. I was given
>   life that I might enjoy all things.

I got nothing I asked for but everything I had hoped
for . . .
Almost despite myself my unspoken prayers were
answered. I am among all men most richly blessed.[1]

Sometimes we feel like God is *not* answering our prayers,
when in reality He is just answering them in a different way than
we expected. Take a moment to reflect on prayers you felt have
gone unanswered—perhaps God did answer them, only in a different way.

FURTHER FATHOMS

• How does James 1:2-4 fit with today's poem?
• In what areas of your life could you use an attitude check?

POWERFUL PRAISE

*God is our shelter and strength, always ready to help in times of trouble. So we
will not be afraid, even if the earth is shaken and mountains fall into the ocean
depths; even if the seas roar and rage, and the hills are shaken by the violence.
There is a river that brings joy to the city of God, to the sacred house of the Most
High. God is in that city, and it will never be destroyed; at early dawn he will
come to its aid. "Stop fighting," he says, "and know that I am God, supreme
among the nations, supreme over the world."*

PSALM 46:1-5,10

RAPID RECAP

• God hears our prayers.
• Sometimes His answers are not the answers we wanted
to hear.

WEEK 6

KEEPING YOUR FOCUS

But they who wait for the LORD shall renew their strength, they shall mount up with wings like eagles, they shall run and not be weary, they shall walk and not faint.

ISAIAH 40:31, RSV

TAKING LESSONS FROM THE MASTER

Therefore, since we are surrounded by such a great cloud of witnesses, let us throw off everything that hinders and the sin that so easily entangles, and let us run with perseverance the race marked out for us. Let us fix our eyes on Jesus, the author and perfecter of our faith, who for the joy set before him endured the cross, scorning its shame, and sat down at the right hand of the throne of God. Consider him who endured such opposition from sinful men, so that you will not grow weary and lose heart.

HEBREWS 12:1-3

A man took his hang glider out on a turbulent day. Wisdom should have told him not to, but his eagerness for his new hobby drew him into the air. All went well for the first part of this trip. Then it hit—a sudden change in the airflow sent his small craft barreling toward Earth. He began to pray, sensing that he was about to crash. At this point, he had no earthly idea of how to pull out of the downdraft. Then, out of the corner of his eye, he saw an eagle caught in the same draft. He watched the eagle's responses. The eagle, with spread wings, seemed to be diving into the ground. Without a moment of hesitation he, too, aimed toward the ground. In a few short flashes of time both he and the eagle had miraculously pulled out of the draft. Because the man knew he could do nothing to save himself, he simply followed the example of the one who knew more than he knew.

This illustration is not unlike what we as Christians can do when it comes to life. There are often moments in our lives when it seems like our world is crashing around us. At those moments we must fix our eyes on Jesus. He is our example, our very life and our breath. He is the reason we exist.

Those who live life to the fullest keep their eyes fixed on Jesus, the author of life.

FURTHER FATHOMS

- What is the message of Hebrews 12:1-3?
- Why is it so easy to remove our focus from Jesus Christ and slip through life on a lower level of faith?

POWERFUL PRAISE

To you, O LORD, I offer my prayer; in you, my God, I trust. Save me from the shame of defeat; don't let my enemies gloat over me! Defeat does not come to those who trust in you, but to those who are quick to rebel against you. Teach me your ways, O LORD; make them known to me. Teach me to live according to your truth, for you are my God, who saves me. I always trust in you. Remember, O LORD, your kindness and constant love which you have shown from long ago.

PSALM 25:1-6

RAPID RECAP

- At times when our world crashes in around us, we must keep our eyes fixed on Jesus.
- Jesus will show us a way even when there seems to be none.

PRESSING ON

*Do you not know that in a race all the runners run, but only one gets the
prize? Run in such a way as to get the prize. Everyone who competes in the
games goes into strict training. They do it to get a crown that will not last;
but we do it to get a crown that will last forever. Therefore I do not run like
a man running aimlessly; I do not fight like a man beating the air. No,
I beat my body and make it my slave so that after I have preached to others,
I myself will not be disqualified for the prize.*

1 CORINTHIANS 9:24-27

I'm a runner—but not Olympic quality. In fact, maybe I shouldn't
call myself a runner. I run. Most of the time I even enjoy running! It started when I was 16. The minister at my church challenged us to write down some goals for life. I still don't know
why I did this but I wrote down that I wanted to run a marathon.
At the time I had never even driven 26.2 miles—let alone run that
distance.

I did absolutely nothing toward that goal for about 20 years.
Then one day I woke up and told my wife, Cathy, I wanted to run
in the Los Angeles Marathon. She laughed. Ouch! I went to the
store and bought expensive running shoes, running shorts, running socks and a headband, but I didn't have time to run. The
next day I ran a mile. Can I be honest? I hated it. The problem
was that I had spent a lot of money on running gear and told

half the world I was going to compete in this marathon. Almost every day after that, I ran and eventually I almost enjoyed some of those days.

Two months before the marathon, my longest run had only been 10 miles. The day I went that far I thought I was going to pass out! I had to really move into high gear if I was going to make it through a marathon. I kept on keeping on, mile after mile, day after day. OK, so there were days my wife, Cathy, pushed me out the door.

All of a sudden the day of the marathon arrived. It was just me and 15,000 other people. Wow! If they could do it, so could I. My goal was to finish—in one day. The first 13 miles were a breeze. At mile 15, I caught a glimpse of Cathy and my girls cheering me on. *No sweat, this marathon goal was easy.* At mile 17, I ate an orange. Immediately I wanted to vomit, use the bathroom, sleep and stop! In fact, I was seriously considering doing all of the above at the same time. I hurt. I took my pulse and found some positive news. I wasn't dead. So I slowed my pace and kept going. I don't remember miles 17 through 22. Then for some reason all my practice paid off. I got my second wind and coasted to the finish line, where bands were playing and my family was cheering.

The first words out of my mouth were, "I never want to do this again!" I was tired. I was sore. I was in pain. I was sweating! After a brief rest, my feelings changed from exhaustion to pure excitement. My months of practice had paid off. It worked. Discipline works. I think I'll go take a nap and then try it again.

God wants us to keep on keeping on. He doesn't ask us to do great and grand things for His kingdom. He asks us to be consistent and faithful. A consistent, faithful person is the one who gets more accomplished over the long haul.

FURTHER FATHOMS

- In what area of your life is God challenging you not to give up?
- What is the point Paul is making in 1 Corinthians 9:24-27?

POWERFUL PRAISE

The LORD is righteous in all he does, merciful in all his acts. He is near to those who call to him, who call to him with sincerity. He supplies the needs of those who honor him; he hears their cries and saves them. He protects everyone who loves him, but he will destroy the wicked. I will always praise the LORD; let all his creatures praise his holy name forever.

PSALM 145:17-21

RAPID RECAP

- Running the race takes preparation.
- God wants us to keep on keeping on.

WHAT WILL YOU DO WITH JESUS?

Very early in the morning, the chief priests, with the elders, the teachers of the law and the whole Sanhedrin, reached a decision. They bound Jesus, led him away and handed him over to Pilate. "Are you the king of the Jews?" asked Pilate. "Yes, it is as you say," Jesus replied.

MARK 15:1-2

Today I want to introduce you to Barabbas. Strange name and a pretty questionable character: a murderer, a thief, a guy who may have walked away from his family. He was evil, filthy scum.

Smelly and vile, Barabbas sat in a dark dungeon waiting to die. Absolutely no one was going to miss him. The next day Barabbas was going to hang on a cross and literally no one would care. Most people would say, "Finally, he's getting what he deserves. He deserves every bit of pain and humiliation on the cross."

Unbeknownst to him while he sat in prison waiting to die, something else was about to happen to him.

"It was the custom at the Feast to release a prisoner whom the people requested" (Mark 15:6). People in the crowd asked Pilate to release someone. "'Do you want me to release to you the king of the Jews?' asked Pilate, knowing it was out of envy that the chief priests had handed Jesus over to him. But the chief priests stirred up the crowd to have Pilate release Barabbas instead. 'What shall I do, then, with the one you call the king of the Jews?' Pilate asked them. 'Crucify him!' they shouted. 'Why? What crime has he committed?' asked Pilate. But they shouted all the louder, 'Crucify him!' Wanting to satisfy the crowd, Pilate released Barabbas to them. He had Jesus flogged, and handed him over to be crucified" (Mark 15:9-15).

The crowd chose Barabbas! Jesus, kind man, miracle worker, healer, friend of children, had hurt no one. Yet the crowd chose Barabbas.

Pilate asked a key question to the crowd who had just a few days before honored Jesus on what we call Palm Sunday. "What will you do with Jesus, the one you call the King of the Jews?"

And the crowd yelled "Crucify him!"

Even Pilate was totally confused and asked, "Why, what crime has he committed?" But they shouted all the louder, "Crucify him." Jesus was whipped, spit on, mocked and turned over to be crucified.

I've always wondered what was going on in the mind of Barabbas when he was set free and Jesus was hung on a cross. He probably heard Pilate's words, "What will you do with Jesus?"

I wonder what decision Barabbas made. His very destiny, life eternal and abundant life on Earth, depended on his response to the single phrase of a Roman leader who in confusion asked a single question: "What will you do with Jesus?"

How about you? What is your response today? What will you do with Jesus?

FURTHER FATHOMS

- What do you think you might have done if you were in the crowd who was yelling for Barabbas?

- What do you think should have been Barabbas's response?

POWERFUL PRAISE

Praise the LORD, the God of Israel! He alone does these wonderful things. Praise his glorious name forever! May his glory fill the whole world. Amen! Amen!

PSALM 72:18-19

RAPID RECAP

- We each must decide what we will do with Jesus who died on the cross.

OBEDIENCE

Whoever has my commands and obeys them, he is the one
who loves me. He who loves me will be loved by my Father, and
I too will love him and show myself to him.

JOHN 14:21

The call to Christ is the call to obedience. Dietrich Bonhoeffer once said, "Only those who obey can believe, and only those who believe can obey."[1]

So many people today have the wrong opinion of living a life of obedience. Obedience is not a penalty levied on faith. It is the strength of faith. The commands of God are all designed to make us happier than we can possibly be without them. The commands of God are not oppressive; they are blessings. Scripture points out that the more we obey God, the more real God becomes to us and the more our faith grows.

The more we love God, the more we become like Him in our characteristics. It is like a good marriage: People who love their spouse want to please him or her; if they do not want to please their spouse, they can hardly talk of loving him or her.

Obedience to God is our loving response to His gifts of life and love. We don't have to obey God out of deep-rooted responsibility; rather, we do it out of a response to what He has already done for us. To obey God is to love God. Jesus said it this way: "If you love me, you will obey what I command" (John 14:15).

Make it a priority to mentally wear a WWJD (What Would Jesus Do?) bracelet as you make decisions this week. See if some of your choices change.

FURTHER FATHOMS

- What is the principle found in John 14:21?
- What areas of your life could use a little more obedience?

POWERFUL PRAISE

As a father is kind to his children, so the LORD is kind to those who honor him. He knows what we are made of; he remembers that we are dust. As for us, our life is like grass. We grow and flourish like a wild flower; then the wind blows on it, and it is gone—no one sees it again. But for those who honor the LORD, his love lasts forever, and his goodness endures for all generations of those who are true to his covenant and who faithfully obey his commands. The LORD placed his throne in heaven; he is king over all. Praise the LORD, you strong and mighty angels, who obey his commands, who listen to what he says. Praise the LORD, all you heavenly powers, you servants of his, who do his will! Praise the LORD, all his creatures in all the places he rules. Praise the LORD, my soul!

PSALM 103:13-22

RAPID RECAP

- If we believe, we will obey.
- If we love Jesus, we will want to obey Him.

NEVER GIVE UP!

*Being confident of this, that he who began a good work in you will carry
it on to completion until the day of Christ Jesus.*

PHILIPPIANS 1:6

In 1491, Christopher Columbus was 40 (that was old back
then!), broke and homeless. Columbus was an outstanding sea
captain—but nobody took very seriously his idea of sailing west
with the hope of discovering a new route to the West Indies.
Nonetheless, Columbus didn't give up.

He once wrote, "Our LORD made me skilled in seamanship,
equipped me with the sciences of astronomy, geometry and
arithmetic, and taught my mind and hand to draw this sphere . . .
then our LORD revealed to me that it was feasible to sail from
here to the Indies and placed in me a burning desire to carry out
this plan."[1]

Five centuries ago, people had a map that reflected their
understanding of the world at that time. It wasn't changed until
the courageous Columbus challenged conventional wisdom by
sailing to the West Indies. His "never give up" attitude resulted
in one of the most significant breakthroughs in world history.

Winston Churchill (a great political statesman of Great
Britain) was once invited to speak to his alma mater. Churchill,
by then one of the most famous men in the world and also one of
the world's greatest orators, had done very poorly at this school.

He approached the podium. All the boys were sitting up straight, totally quiet, waiting for great words of wisdom. Churchill stood behind the podium looking in the eyes of each boy. Then he quietly said, "Never give up." He stared at them again and shouted, "Never give up." He pounded the podium and at the top of his voice he screamed, "Never, never, never give up!"[2] Winston Churchill then sat down. His speech was made up of just one piece of advice: Never give up.

I'm not sure what exactly you are going through but this I know: The people who make a difference in the world and in their own lives never give up.

FURTHER FATHOMS

- How does Philippians 1:6 relate to you?
- Who is an example of someone you know who has never given up?

POWERFUL PRAISE

Praise the LORD, all nations! Praise him, all peoples! His love for us is strong, and his faithfulness is eternal. Praise the LORD!

PSALM 117

RAPID RECAP

- Never give up.
- Never give up!

GO FOR IT

For if you give, you will get! Your gift will return to you in full and overflowing measure, pressed down, shaken together to make room for more, and running over. Whatever measure you use to give—large or small—will be used to measure what is given back to you.

LUKE 6:38, *TLB*

The call to Christ is the call to serve. Sometimes our servant-hood is not appreciated; at other times we serve when no one notices. Nevertheless, we are called to serve. Some years ago Kent M. Keith put together what he calls the Paradoxical Commandments. I like them and keep them close to my heart.

People are illogical, unreasonable, and self-centered.
Love them anyway.
If you do good, people will accuse you of selfish ulterior motives.
Do good anyway.
If you are successful, you win false friends and true enemies.
Succeed anyway.
The good you do today will be forgotten tomorrow.
Do good anyway.
Honesty and frankness make you vulnerable.
Be honest and frank anyway.

The biggest men and women with the biggest ideas can be shot down by the smallest men and women with the smallest minds.

Think big anyway.

People favor underdogs but follow only top dogs.

Fight for a few underdogs anyway.

What you spend years building may be destroyed overnight.

Build anyway.

People really need help but may attack you if you do help them.

Help people anyway.

Give the world the best you have and you'll get kicked in the teeth.

Give the world the best you have anyway.[1]

FURTHER FATHOMS

- How can Luke 6:27-31 relate to your life?
- What can you do to become a more effective servant of God?

POWERFUL PRAISE

Happy are those who have reverence for the Lord, who live by his commands. Your work will provide for your needs; you will be happy and prosperous.

PSALM 128:12

RAPID RECAP

- The call to Christ is the call to serve.
- We must go forward in our call, even when we are not noticed or not appreciated.

WAITING

But they who wait for the LORD shall renew their strength, they shall mount up with wings like eagles, they shall run and not be weary, they shall walk and not faint.

ISAIAH 40:31, *RSV*

I've been learning a lot about waiting. I don't like to wait and I don't wait very well. I'm the guy who cuts across the grass to get there faster. When there is a line at the market, I watch for another check-stand to open and try to get there first. When I played baseball, I wouldn't wait on the curve ball, and in track I'd jump the gun at the start.

My friend Don Springer taught me a good lesson about waiting. I love to snorkel. There is almost nothing I would rather do than swim in the clear blue waters of the world looking at tropical fish, coral and the underwater world. (Okay, so you think I'm strange!)

Don and I went snorkeling in Napili Bay, Maui, Hawaii. Don is a retired fireman who also likes to snorkel. He drove me crazy. He couldn't swim for six feet without stopping for minutes at a time.

But a funny thing happened when I would stop long enough to wait for Don. I saw more fish, more eels, more movements in the water than I had ever seen before in my life. Don taught me to stop, look and listen in the water. Although I'd snorkeled at Napili Bay before, I had never truly experienced Napili Bay until

Don showed me how to wait.

It's a good lesson for life. Maybe we should quit rushing around trying to find God. Maybe we should stop, look, listen and wait. He's here. He has something to reveal and say to you today.

FURTHER FATHOMS

- Read Psalm 27:14. What's the message to you in this psalm?
- In what areas of your life do you have a difficulty with waiting?

POWERFUL PRAISE

I waited patiently for the LORD's help; then he listened to me and heard my cry. He pulled me out of a dangerous pit, out of the deadly quicksand. He set me safely on a rock and made me secure. He taught me to sing a new song, a song of praise to our God. Many who see this will take warning and will put their trust in the LORD.

PSALM 40:1-3

RAPID RECAP

- God wants us to wait on Him.
- When we wait on God, we see more of who He is.

WEEK 7

GETTING IT TOGETHER

But seek first his kingdom and his righteousness,
all these things will be given to you as well.

MATTHEW 6:33

STANDING AT THE DOOR

Here I am! I stand at the door and knock. If anyone hears my voice and opens the door, I will come in and eat with him, and he with me.

REVELATION 3:20

I have a picture in my mind whenever I hear Revelation 3:20. It is a picture of Jesus standing at a door knocking, but the door can only be opened from the inside because there is no doorknob on the outside of the door.

When Jesus knocks at the door of our heart, we basically have four options:

1. **Reject Him**. There are some people who have turned their backs on God. God says, "I love you," and they say, "I want nothing to do with You." A young college student once told me, "I reject Jesus Christ." It broke my heart, and I have a feeling it broke God's heart, too.

2. **Ignore Him.** The people who do this think that they have heard it all. They know the words of the gospel but the message goes in one ear and out the other. Some of these people say, "Later, LORD." They

make excuses such as "I'm yours, God, as soon as I get out of school or break up with my boyfriend or get married or get that promotion" or whatever it is that rules their hearts. The excuses just keep on coming.

3. **Appease Him.** We all know people like this. They're all around us. They go through the motions but really don't allow Christ to change their lives. They often go to church. They sit, observe, say the right stuff at the right time and then do nothing about it. Here's what Christ said about them (and these aren't pleasant words):

> So, because you are *lukewarm*—neither hot nor cold—I am about to spit you out of my mouth (Rev. 3:16, emphasis added).

4. **Obey Him.** I hope you fall into this category. People like this, although not perfect, fully desire to live for God. These Christians have made Jesus the master of their lives. He is their Savior and LORD. They say, "I'm yours, LORD, and I want to obey you."

Here's a great promise for those who choose option 4:

Whoever has my commands and obeys them, he is the one who loves me. He who loves me will be loved by my Father, and I too will love him and show myself to him (John 14:21).

Which option have you chosen?

FURTHER FATHOMS

- What is the spiritual principle found in John 14-21?
- Which part of your life do you see Jesus still knocking on?

POWERFUL PRAISE

I praise you, LORD, because you have saved me and kept my enemies from gloat-ing over me. I cried to you for help, O LORD my God, and you healed me; you kept me from the grave. I was on my way to the depths below, but you restored my life. Sing praise to the LORD, all his faithful people! Remember what the Holy One has done, and give him thanks! His anger lasts only a moment, his goodness for a lifetime. Tears may flow in the night, but joy comes in the morning.

PSALM 30:1-5

RAPID RECAP

- Jesus stands at the door and knocks.
- We can choose to reject, ignore, appease or obey Him.

PUT GOD FIRST

Therefore I tell you, do not worry about your life, what you will eat or drink; or about your body, what you will wear. Is not life more important than food, and the body more important than clothes? Look at the birds of the air; they do not sow or reap or store away in barns, and yet your heavenly Father feeds them. Are you not much more valuable than they? Who of you by worrying can add a single hour to his life?

And why do you worry about clothes? See how the lilies of the field grow. They do not labor or spin. Yet I tell you that not even Solomon in all his splendor was dressed like one of these. If that is how God clothes the grass of the field, which is here today and tomorrow is thrown into the fire, will he not much more clothe you, O you of little faith? So do not worry, saying, "What shall we eat?" or "What shall we drink?" or "What shall we wear?" For the pagans run after all these things, and your heavenly Father knows that you need them. But seek first his kingdom and his righteousness, and all these things will be given to you as well.

MATTHEW 6:25-33

There is a scene in the movie *Chariots of Fire* that is forever etched in my mind. The movie tells the story of Eric Liddell. He went to the 1924 Summer Olympics in Paris, France, and was slated to run in the 100-yard dash competition on a Sunday. There was only one problem: This incredible athlete took his faith more seriously than his running. For Liddell, his faith in God told him he could not run on a Sunday. All efforts to persuade him otherwise failed. A British dignitary finally cried out in frustration, "What a pity we couldn't have persuaded him to run." After a moment's pause his coach responded, "It would have been a pity if we had, because we would have separated him from the source of his speed."[1]

Eric Liddell's obedience to his faith was his source of strength and purpose. His firm stand for God helped him to be one of the great, inspiring athletes of the twentieth century.

How about you? Is your desire to serve Jesus greater than your other desires? Today is a good day to take another look at your priorities. I've never met a person who put God first in his or her life who ever regretted it.

FURTHER FATHOMS

- What can you do to put God first in your life?
- What makes Matthew 6:33 such a significant Scripture for Christians?

POWERFUL PRAISE

The king is glad, O LORD, because you gave him strength; he rejoices because you made him victorious. You have given him his heart's desire; you have answered his request. You came to him with great blessings and set a crown of gold on his head. He asked for life, and you gave it, a long and lasting life. His glory is great because of your help; you have given him fame and majesty. Your blessings are with him forever, and your presence fills him with joy. The king trusts in the LORD Almighty; and because of the LORD's constant love he will always be secure.

PSALM 21:1-7

RAPID RECAP

- God is our source.
- We must put our faith first in our lives.

NEW LIFE

*In reply Jesus declared, "I tell you the truth, no one can see the
kingdom of God unless he is born again."*

JOHN 3:3

When I was in Hawaii, I witnessed a baptism like none I've ever
seen before. First, the location: Kapalua Beach, Maui. They call it
the most beautiful beach in the United States, with its crystal-
clear water, sugary white sand and a view that helps me understand the definition of "breathtaking."

Second, the people. My favorite church in the world is
Kumulani Chapel. Believe it or not, the congregation meets in a
golf-cart shed every Sunday morning in Kapalua, Maui. Some
people come in aloha shirts and dresses, others wear more tradi-
tional clothes. There are older saints sitting next to surfers (with
their hair still wet from riding a wave just minutes before the
start of the service).

Today after the service, the people got into their cars, many
with surfboards strapped on the top, and drove to the beach to
have church again. They sang, they prayed, they praised God.
Pastor Mark explained that baptism was the sign of new life in
Jesus Christ. It symbolized the washing away of our sins and the
beginning of life with Christ as our Savior. Some of the people
(young and old) were still wearing church clothes, while others
were in swimsuits. As those being baptized waded out into the

clear blue water, the congregation sang songs of praise:

Our God is an awesome God.
He reigns from heaven above
with wisdom, power and love.
Our God is an awesome God.[1]

And Jesus said, "Come to the water, stand by my side.
I know you are thirsty, you won't be denied.
I felt every tear drop, when in darkness you cried.
And I strove to remind you that for those tears I died."[2]

As each person was baptized the congregation cheered, clapped, even whistled! Then, when each person reached dry sand, that newly-baptized saint was greeted with one bear hug after another. No one seemed to worry about getting wet from those hugs—in fact, I'm not sure anyone noticed. Everyone sang some more and prayed some more, and then it was time to cheer for the next person. Although I didn't see the physical body of Jesus, I sensed His presence. I had this feeling He was there—and I even had this suspicion that He was the first to cheer and whistle. After all, He gave the new life, and He was the reason everyone came and many were baptized.

FURTHER FATHOMS

- Although various traditions baptize people in different ways, there is always a great deal of meaning behind this experience. What does your baptism mean to you?
- According to John 3:3, why did John baptize people? What makes this practice good news?

POWERFUL PRAISE

Praise the LORD!
Praise God in his Temple! Praise his strength in heaven!
Praise him for the mighty things he has done. Praise
his supreme greatness.
Praise him with trumpets. Praise him with harps and lyres.
Praise him with drums and dancing. Praise him
with harps and flutes.
Praise him with cymbals. Praise him with loud cymbals.
Praise the LORD, all living creatures!
Praise the LORD!

PSALM 150

RAPID RECAP

- God wants us to be baptized when we believe.
- Baptism is an outward gesture of the new life we have in Christ.

NEW BEGINNINGS

If we confess our sins, he is faithful and just and will forgive us our sins and
purify us from all unrighteousness.

1 JOHN 1:9

At a conference of governors several years ago, an interesting question was raised: What is the greatest thing in the world? It was absolutely quiet. None of the governors had an answer. Finally a young aide took the microphone and said, "The greatest thing in the world is that we can walk away from yesterday."[1]

I'm not even sure if that young aide knew that she had just summarized the essence of the gospel of Jesus Christ. The good news of the Christian faith is that we can walk away from yesterday. The apostle Paul could walk away from his persecution of Christians and answer the call to Christ (see Acts 9). The woman caught in adultery could walk away from her destructive lifestyle into a new journey with Jesus Christ (see John 8). Matthew could walk away from his job as a crooked tax collector and follow Christ into a new life (see Mark 2:14). The prodigal son could walk away from his life of moral failures in the far country and walk into the loving, forgiving arms of his father (see Luke 15).

To walk away from the failures and guilt of yesterday rests at the very heart of forgiveness. This is no call to cop out, drop out or otherwise escape responsibility or the consequences of our choices. But it is a liberating message that no one, absolutely no one, is tied to a past from which there is no release. The gospel gladly sings of the possibility of new beginnings. Aren't you glad you have been released from your past?

FURTHER FATHOMS

- Read David's psalm of forgiveness: Psalm 51. What are the results of his confession of sin?
- In what areas of your life do you need a new beginning? List these areas and pray for forgiveness according to 1 John 1:9.

POWERFUL PRAISE

Be merciful to me, O God, because of your constant love. Because of your great mercy wipe away my sins! Wash away all my evil and make me clean from my sin! Remove my sin, and I will be clean; wash me, and I will be whiter than snow. Let me hear the sounds of joy and gladness; and though you have crushed me and broken me, I will be happy once again. Close your eyes to my sins and wipe out all my evil. Create a pure heart in me, O God, and put a new and loyal spirit in me. Do not banish me from your presence; do not take your holy spirit away from me. Give me again the joy that comes from your salvation, and make me willing to obey you.

PSALM 51:1-2,7-12

RAPID RECAP

- In Jesus, we are not bound by what we did yesterday.
- We can have a new beginning.

MAKING PEACE

For if you forgive men when they sin against you, your heavenly
Father will also forgive you. But if you do not forgive men their sins,
your Father will not forgive your sins.

MATTHEW 6:14-15

Leonardo da Vinci painted one of the great masterpieces in the history of the world. This work of art is called *The Last Supper.* Few people know the story behind the creation of this famous painting.

Da Vinci had an enemy who was also a painter. Right before da Vinci began to paint this picture of Jesus with His disciples, he had a bitter argument with his enemy. When da Vinci painted the face of Judas Iscariot, he used the face of his enemy as a reference so that his enemy would be present for ages as the man who betrayed Jesus. While painting this picture, da Vinci took delight in knowing that others would actually notice the face of his enemy on Judas.

He continued painting the faces of the other disciples and often tried to paint the face of Jesus, but he could not make any progress. Da Vinci was frustrated and confused. In time, he realized what was wrong. His hatred for the other painter was holding him back from finishing the face of Jesus. Only after making peace with his fellow painter and repainting the face of Judas was he able to paint the face of Jesus and complete his masterpiece.[1]

Is there a broken relationship in your life that needs mending? Pray that God will give you courage to take the next step toward reconciliation.

- What was the lesson Leonardo da Vinci learned?
- Is there someone in your life you need to forgive to make peace with God and that person?

POWERFUL PRAISE

From the depths of my despair I call to you, LORD. Hear my cry, O LORD; listen to my call for help! If you kept a record of our sins, who could escape being condemned? But you forgive us, so that we should reverently obey you. I wait eagerly for the LORD's help, and in his word I trust. I wait for the LORD more eagerly than sentries wait for the dawn—than sentries wait for the dawn.

PSALM 130:1-6

RAPID RECAP

- When we hold hate for an enemy, it can get in the way of completing what God has called us to complete.
- We must be willing to ask forgiveness and mend broken relationships.

DON'T STOP—
DON'T QUIT

He will keep you strong to the end, so that you will be blameless on the day of our LORD Jesus Christ. God, who has called you into fellowship with his Son Jesus Christ our LORD, is faithful.

1 CORINTHIANS 1:8-9

Today's story is for those who, like myself, at times get discouraged with their progress in their spiritual life. Don't stop; don't quit. God will help you with the power of His Holy Spirit.

A story is told about a famous composer-pianist who was scheduled to perform at a great concert hall in America. It was an evening to remember—black tuxedos and long evening dresses, a high society extravaganza. Present in the audience that evening was a mother with her fidgety nine-year-old son. Weary of waiting, the little boy squirmed in his seat. His mother was hoping that her boy would be encouraged to practice the piano if he could just hear the immortal pianist at the keyboard. So, against the little boy's wishes, he had come.

As the mother turned to talk with friends, her son decided that he could stay seated no longer. He slipped away from her side, strangely drawn to the ebony concert grand Steinway and its leather tufted stool on the huge stage flooded with blinding lights. Without much notice from the sophisticated audience, the boy sat down at the stool, staring wide-eyed at the black and white keys. He placed his small, trembling fingers in the right location and began to play "Chopsticks." The roar of the crowd was hushed as hundreds of frowning faces turned in his direction. Irritated and embarrassed, they began to shout: "Get that boy away from there!" "Who'd bring a kid that young in here?" "Where's his mother?" "Somebody stop him!"

Backstage, the master overheard the sounds out front and quickly put together in his mind what was happening. Hurriedly, he grabbed his coat and rushed toward the stage. Without one word of announcement he stooped over behind the stool, reached around the boy, and began to improvise a countermelody to harmonize with and enhance the boy's rendition of "Chopsticks." As the two of them played together, the famous pianist kept whispering in the boy's ear "Keep going. Don't quit, son. Keep playing. Don't stop . . . don't quit."[1]

God is the maestro who improvises a countermelody and enhances our efforts. Like a master pianist, He whispers in our ears, "Don't stop. Don't give up." He encourages us to continue, even when our efforts appear small—especially in the eyes of others (or how we think others see our efforts).

FURTHER FATHOMS

- Have you ever felt like giving up? How does this story inspire you to keep on going?
- According to Philippians 1:6 and 1 Corinthians 1:8-9, what is God's job in your life?

POWERFUL PRAISE

I thank you, LORD, with all my heart; I sing praise to you before the gods. I face your holy Temple, bow down, and praise your name because of your constant love and faithfulness, because you have shown that your name and your commands are supreme. You answered me when I called to you; with your strength you strengthened me. All the kings in the world will praise you, LORD, because they have heard your promises. They will sing about what you have done and about your great glory. Even though you are so high above, you care for the lowly, and the proud cannot hide from you. When I am surrounded by troubles, you keep me safe. You oppose my angry enemies and save me by your power. You will do everything you have promised; LORD, your love is eternal. Complete the work that you have begun.

PSALM 138

RAPID RECAP

- God wants us to keep going forward.
- When we do, He will be there to turn our efforts into a masterpiece.

MENDING THE BROKEN PARTS

Every good and perfect gift is from above, coming down from the Father of the heavenly lights, who does not change like shifting shadows.

JAMES 1:17

He had only one eye and his arm was dangling by a thread. But four-year-old Hannah loved Bear. Bear always accompanied her to Sunday School. One day her teacher suggested that the class pray for people who were sick and hurting. The children prayed for hungry children around the world, sick relatives and broken relationships. Hannah put her arms around poor, tattered Bear. She prayed, "Dear Jesus, please make Bear better."

Then Hannah had such a good time at church, she forgot Bear and left without him. One of Hannah's teachers had heard her prayer and took Bear home to "heal" him. She replaced both eyes with pretty new buttons and sewed the arm back on. When she returned Bear to Hannah, Hannah was filled with joy. "God fixed Bear," she said.

What Hannah would later understand about God is that sometimes He heals directly; other times He uses people like her Sunday School teacher to sew our bears together and help mend the broken parts of our lives.

FURTHER FATHOMS

- When has God used someone in your life to help you with a burden?
- What characteristic of God do you see in James 1:17 and Matthew 7:11?

POWERFUL PRAISE

Show us your constant love, O LORD, and give us your saving help. I am listening to what the LORD God is saying; he promises peace to us, his own people, if we do not go back to our foolish ways. Surely he is ready to save those who honor him, and his saving presence will remain in our land. Love and faithfulness will meet; righteousness and peace will embrace. Human loyalty will reach up from the earth, and God's righteousness will look down from heaven. The LORD will make us prosperous, and our land will produce rich harvests. Righteousness will go before the LORD and prepare the path for him.

PSALM 85:7-13

RAPID RECAP

- God will heal our hurts.
- Sometimes He will use others to do the healing and sometimes He will use us to help heal others.

ENDNOTES

Week 2
Sunday
1. Source unknown.

Tuesday
1. Cary Grant, quoted in "Dear Abby," November 29, 1991, "The Ultimate Cary Grant Pages," *carygrant.net.* http://search.netscape.com/ns/boom frame.jsp?query=Cary+Grant+and+meditation&page=1&offset=0&result _url=redir%3Fsrc%3Dwebsearch%26amp%3BrequestId%3D3c0beb455d8 7db4f%26amp%3BclickedItemRank%3D1%26amp%3BuserQuery%3DCar y%2BGrant%2Band%2Bmeditation%26amp%3BclickedItemURN%3Dhtt p%253A%252F%252Fwww.carygrant.net%252Farticles%252Fdearabby.ht m%26amp%3BinvocationType%3D%26amp%3BfromPage%3DAppleTop &remove_url=http%3A%2F%2Fwww.carygrant.net%2Farticles%2Fdearab by.htm (accessed February 23, 2004).

Week 3
Sunday
1. *Guideposts* (December 1989), p. 28.
2. Ibid.

Monday
1. *Jehova-Rapha* is one of the names for God in the Old Testament (see Exod.

15:26) and it means "the LORD who heals."

Tuesday
1. Source unknown.

Wednesday
1. Child Abuse Prevention Program (CAPP), Orange, CA.
2. Ibid.

Thursday
1. Author's personal collection.
2. Graduate School of Education at Northern Illinois University, DeKalb, IL.

Friday
1. "The Houses that Prayer Built," *Christian History Institute*. http://www.gospelcom.net/chi/GLIMPSEF/child/glch008.shtml (accessed April 15, 2004).

Saturday
1. "San Francisco Earthquake History 1915-1989," *The Virtual Museum of the City of San Francisco*. http://www.sfmuseum.org/alm/quakes3.html (accessed April 16, 2004).

Week 4
Wednesday
1. Samuel Morse, quoted in "Glimpses," issue 99 (Worcester, PA: Christian History Institute, 1998), n.p.
2. Ibid.

Thursday
1. C. Sumner Wemp, "One Soul Leads to Another," *American Tract Society*. http://www.atstracts.org/devotionals/devotional_archive.php?file=68.txt (accessed April 30, 2004).

Week 5
Tuesday
1. Dale Wasserman, Joe Darion and Mitch Leigh, *Man of La Mancha*.
2. Johann Wolfgang von Goethe, "Expectations Quotes," *Wisdom Quotes*. http://www.wisdomquotes.com/cat_expectations.html (accessed April 30, 2004).

Wednesday
1. Source unknown.

Thursday
1. "Facts About Terry," *The Terry Fox Foundation.* http://www.terryfoxrun.org/english/terry%20fox/facts/default.asp?s=1 (accessed April 30, 2004).

Friday
1. Willard A. Peterson, "Slow Me Down."

Saturday
1. Unknown Confederate soldier, quoted by John P. Jumper, "Honoring a Hero," *Air Force Link.* http://www.af.mil/speech/speech.asp?speechID=63 (accessed April 30, 2004).

Week 6
Wednesday
1. Dietrich Bonhoeffer, *The Cost of Discipleship* (Carmichael, CA: Touchstone Books, 1995), n.p.

Thursday
1. Source unknown.
2. Winston Churchill, quoted in Sherwood Elliot Wirt and Kersten Beckstrom, *Topical Encyclopedia of Living Quotations* (Minneapolis, MN: Bethany House Publishers, 1982), p. 172.

Friday
1. Kent M. Keith, "The Paradoxical Commandments." © Copyright Kent M. Keith 1968, renewed 2001. Used by permission.

Week 7
Monday
1. Source unknown.

Tuesday
1. Rich Mullins, "Awesome God." © 1988 BMG Songs, Inc. (ASCAP).
2. Marsha J. Stevens, "For Those Tears I Died."

Wednesday

1. Source unknown.

Thursday

1. "Leonardo da Vinci," *Story of Love.* http://www.alphatec.or.jp/~fvw/eng lish/story/vinci.htm (accessed May 4, 2004).

Friday

1. This story has been widely told about the famous pianist Ignace Jan Paderewski and can be found on many Internet sites. However, truthor fiction.com has challenged its authenticity. Whether truth or fiction, for the purposes of this reading, the point is a good one. For details regarding this story, see http://www.truthorfiction.com/rumors/p/paderewski.htm (accessed April 30, 2004).

More of the Best from Jim Burns

For Parents and Youth Workers

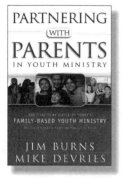

Partnering with Parents in Youth Ministry
The Practical Guide to Today's Family-Based Youth Ministry
ISBN 08307.32292

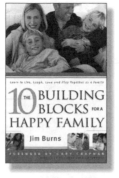

The 10 Building Blocks for a Happy Family
Learn to Live, Laugh, Love and Play Together as a Family
ISBN 08307.33027

The Youth Builder
Reach Young People, Strengthen Families and Change Lives Forever
ISBN 08307.29232

For Teens

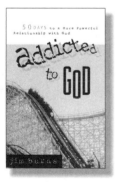

Addicted to God
Fifty Days to a More Powerful Relationship with God
ISBN 08307.25318

No Compromise
A Passionate Devotional to Ignite Your Faith
ISBN 08307.29127

Surviving Adolescence
Learning to Like Yourself and Make Wise Decisions
ISBN 08307.20650